T0265695

BUILD

TO

RENT

CHARLIE KRIEGEL

BUILD TO RENT

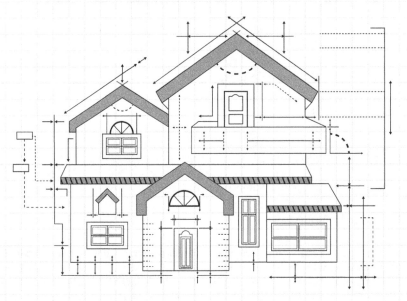

A HOW-TO GUIDE FOR THE INSTITUTIONAL INVESTOR

Forbes | Books

Published by Forbes Books, Charleston, South Carolina.
An imprint of Advantage Media Group.

Forbes Books is a registered trademark, and the Forbes Books colophon is a trademark of Forbes Media, LLC.

Printed in the United States of America.

10 9 8 7 6 5 4 3 2 1

ISBN: 979-8-88750-123-9 (Hardcover)
ISBN: 979-8-88750-124-6 (eBook)

Library of Congress Control Number: 2024915347

Book design by Analisa Smith.

This custom publication is intended to provide accurate information and the opinions of the author in regard to the subject matter covered. It is sold with the understanding that the publisher, Forbes Books, is not engaged in rendering legal, financial, or professional services of any kind. If legal advice or other expert assistance is required, the reader is advised to seek the services of a competent professional.

Since 1917, Forbes has remained steadfast in its mission to serve as the defining voice of entrepreneurial capitalism. Forbes Books, launched in 2016 through a partnership with Advantage Media, furthers that aim by helping business and thought leaders bring their stories, passion, and knowledge to the forefront in custom books. Opinions expressed by Forbes Books authors are their own. To be considered for publication, please visit **books.Forbes.com**.

This book is dedicated to my loving and supportive wife, Vanessa.

CONTENTS

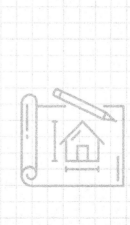

At the helm of WinHill Advisors-Kirby, one of Texas's premier investment brokerages, stands Charlie Kriegel, a distinguished leader in the real estate investment sector. With a rich, decade-long history of navigating the complexities of the market, Charlie has been instrumental in orchestrating the acquisition of single-family properties, amassing a total transaction value exceeding a billion dollars. His expertise and strategic foresight have made him the trusted representative for numerous leading hedge funds, focusing on the burgeoning market of build-to-rent (BTR) communities nationwide, with a keen emphasis on Texas.

Under his guidance, WinHill Advisors-Kirby is currently spearheading the development of four innovative BTR projects within Texas. These ventures, encompassing a total of 263 units, are poised to generate an impressive sales volume of $96 million. Beyond these immediate projects, Charlie's vision extends to the future, with his team actively working on tripling its BTR development sites. These sites are in various stages of securing entitlements and municipal site plan approvals, laying the groundwork for substantial growth and development opportunities.

Charlie's unparalleled commitment to excellence and his profound understanding of the investment landscape have attracted a prestigious clientele. His portfolio of clients includes several industry giants in the BTR space. Through his leadership, WinHill Advisors-Kirby continues to set the standard for innovation and success in the real estate investment industry.

Reflecting on my early days, navigating the bustling real estate market for a prominent hedge fund, I recall the ambitious goal of acquiring approximately one hundred properties each month. These properties, once procured, were promptly transitioned to the fund's property management team for leasing. However, a pivotal moment arose when the sheer volume of properties overwhelmed the team's capacity to lease them efficiently. It was then that my team and I were enlisted to bridge this gap. Embracing a principle that has guided me throughout my career, I adhered to the ethos of never declining a client's request but rather adopting a learn-as-you-go approach to overcome challenges.

This mindset was put to the test one sweltering Saturday in Houston as I embarked on my routine inventory photography across the city. It was a task I approached with meticulous attention to detail, ensuring each property was showcased at its best. Upon exiting one house, I was suddenly besieged by fleas, attacking my ankles and stomach with voracious bites. In a moment of desperation and with little regard for the bustling neighborhood around me, I found myself in a comical yet frantic dance, attempting to rid myself of the pests in what can only be described as a spectacle for the amused onlookers.

This experience, though humorous in hindsight, served as a poignant reminder of the unpredictable and often humbling nature of the real estate business. It underscored the importance of adaptability, resilience, and maintaining a sense of humor in the face of adversity. More importantly, it highlighted the significance of personal sacrifice and dedication to client service—a commitment to do whatever it takes to meet client needs, even if it means working through unconventional challenges.

As I drove away that day, my clothing confined to a trash bag and my dignity slightly tarnished, I was reminded of the broader lessons this industry teaches us. Real estate is more than transactions and properties; it's about facing unexpected obstacles with determination and a willingness to adapt. This ethos has been a cornerstone of my approach to the build-to-rent sector, where flexibility, innovative problem-solving, and an unwavering commitment to excellence have paved the way for success.

Unfortunately, one agent didn't see the posting before showing the home to a family after I left. Needless to say, they were not only eaten by the fleas, but little did we know that there was also a bee colony nested inside the walls of the house. The family was not only chased out of the house by the fleas, but once out in the backyard, they were then attacked by the bees! Ever since, that property has been known as the "Bees and Fleas House." This particular property, forever branded by its unfortunate nickname, symbolizes the kind of unforeseen challenges that can emerge in this line of work.

Yet the narrative of the "Bees and Fleas House" does more than recount an unpredictable ordeal; it sets the stage for a broader discussion on the evolution of the real estate market, particularly the emergence of build-to-rent (BTR) developments. As we transition from these anecdotal experiences to the analysis of BTR developments, it's essential to recognize the complexity and dynamism of the real estate market. BTRs present a novel approach to addressing the growing demand for affordable housing, challenging traditional perceptions of homeownership and its role in the American dream. This shift signifies a considerable transformation affecting all stakeholders in real estate, necessitating a distinct mindset, especially for those of us working with institutional investors. The field demands resilience, adaptability to market fluctuations, and a relentless dedication to navigating the myriad challenges that come our way.

My journey in real estate, initiated in 2004 as the youngest agent in a highly competitive firm, reflects the relentless pursuit and passion that have defined my career. Despite initially lacking the luxury clientele that typifies top producers, my persistence and eagerness to learn from those around me carved out my path in this industry. The firm's decision to give me a chance, driven by my determination not to leave until I was offered a position, exemplifies the mentality I've applied throughout my career. Surrounded by incredible talent, I benefited immensely from coaching and mentoring, which were pivotal in shaping my understanding of the business and honing my skills to serve the sophisticated needs of institutional investors.

This turning point in my career, marked by the partnership with an investor committed to acquiring one to two investment properties monthly, was instrumental in expanding my expertise and influence within the real estate market. The relentless pursuit of foreclosures and distressed properties across the greater Houston area was not just a quest for the next viable investment; it was an invaluable learning experience that laid the groundwork for my comprehensive understanding of the market's intricacies. This period of intensive exploration and discovery was characterized by countless hours spent navigating through diverse neighborhoods, evaluating properties that ranged from fixer-uppers destined for flips to potential additions to a growing rental income portfolio. The vast geography of Houston, with its rich tapestry of communities, provided a unique backdrop for this phase of my career. Each day brought new insights into the characteristics that defined the most promising investment areas—be it their superior school rankings, favorable tax rates, or other desirable attributes that would appeal to potential renters or buyers. The evolution of my business from these early days of chasing foreclosures to becoming a recognized authority in the BTR sector is a testament to the power of persistence, market intelligence, and the ability to adapt to the shifting landscapes of real estate investment. The experience of building a database on the highest-opportunity areas was more than just a methodical accumulation of data; it was the cornerstone upon which WinHill Advisors-Kirby was built, embodying our commitment to informed investment strategies and a deep understanding of the markets we serve.

The journey from spearheading acquisitions of buy-and-hold homes to founding WinHill Advisors epitomizes the essence of innovation and resilience in the real estate sector. Less than a decade ago, the landscape of single-family home acquisitions was markedly different from today's tech-driven environment. The absence of sophisticated algorithms and online platforms to streamline the purchase of single-family homes for rental income presented a unique challenge—a challenge that my team and I embraced wholeheartedly. As pioneers in this space, we collaborated closely with our hedge fund partner to develop a comprehensive database on rental rates and identify the highest-yielding neighborhoods across Texas. This endeavor, marked by the acquisition of over five hundred homes in the greater Houston area within just ten months, solidified our position as leading experts in the single-family rental (SFR) market.

Our success in this venture was not merely a testament to our expertise in real estate acquisitions; it reflected a broader commitment to innovation and strategic foresight. Recognizing the potential of the SFR space, the hedge fund entrusted us with the responsibility of leading a new division. This pivotal moment paved the way for the establishment of WinHill Advisors, a company that would soon become synonymous with leadership in real estate investment and advisory services.

However, the path to success is seldom linear. Six months into our partnership, a significant downturn in oil prices led the fund to withdraw from the market, abruptly halting our property acquisitions. This unforeseen challenge could have been a setback, but instead, it served as a catalyst for growth. Demonstrating agility and resilience, we swiftly pivoted our strategy, diversifying our client base and securing partnerships that remain integral to WinHill Advisors to this day.

This episode in our history underscores a critical lesson: the real estate market is inherently volatile, and success demands both flexibility and the capacity to anticipate and respond to rapid changes. Our ability to pivot in the face of adversity not only ensured our survival but also spurred our evolution, enabling us to emerge stronger and more diversified.

As WinHill Advisors continues to grow and adapt to the ever-changing dynamics of the real estate market, the principles of innovation, resilience, and strategic foresight remain at the core of our operations. These principles have guided us through the challenges and opportunities of the past and will continue to drive our success in the future. Our journey from a pioneering team in the SFR space to the leaders of a thriving real estate advisory firm exemplifies the transformative power of embracing change and leveraging expertise to navigate the complexities of the market.

Today, we work on everything from single-family homes to REOs, fix-and-flips, commercial fix-and-flips, land opportunities for developers, or aligning institutional investors with others interested in providing capital. We also work on a new model known as build-to-rent.

It's been a challenge to explain to others—even those in the real estate industry—this new model. With no seminars, podcasts, or other media attention on this new investment strategy at times, it's been like trying to teach a new language. All of my peers and colleagues assumed working for a hedge fund was a luxurious opportunity, so they've had trouble fathoming the long hours and tough skin it takes to succeed in this particular segment of real estate.

In fact, one of the first perceptions when people hear about BTRs is that it's destroying the American dream of home ownership. Yet, as I write this book, the interest rate increase has taken an estimated 10 million homebuyers out of the market. These people still need somewhere to live, and BTR communities provide that in a house at the same price as an apartment, yet with the amenities that come with being part of a quality neighborhood.

Is BTR taking away the American Dream? Or is it another space within the affordable housing segment? The information in the pages ahead will address these questions and more. I want to show you the benefits of BTR and what it takes to get these projects through to completion. It's a viable option for people who want to rent a home, not just an apartment, and be close to the city and all the amenities of a community—especially in a world where more than 30 percent of single-family homes are owned by investors or at a price point of

$400,000, when most people can only afford a lower price point, and that's where most real estate professionals operate.

Because BTR is a misunderstood concept by many people, and all the rhetoric is making it difficult to get to the truth, I wrote this book to help clarify what this new type of housing and investment is all about. As someone integrally involved in their development, I want to help real estate agents, investors, builders, developers, and anyone interested in investing in commercial or residential real estate see that it's a viable, affordable housing option for today—and tomorrow.

PART I:

WHEN YOU'RE GETTING IN ON THE (LITERAL) GROUND FLOOR

CHAPTER 1

THIS IS HOW 40 PERCENT OF US WILL LIVE

Addressing the evolving landscape of the American dream, particularly in the context of homeownership versus renting, opens a crucial dialogue about the future of housing in the United States. The build-to-rent (BTR) model is at the forefront of this discussion, presenting a modern solution that aligns with the changing priorities and financial realities of many Americans. Despite the common misconception that BTR threatens the traditional dream of owning a home, the current economic climate and housing market trends suggest a different story.

In an era where the cost of homeownership is increasingly out of reach for a significant portion of the population, the financial benefits of renting cannot be overlooked. On average, the monthly expenses associated with owning a home—ranging from $2,883 to $3,759—far exceed the national average rent of $1,372. This disparity highlights a pivotal shift in the housing market, where for many, renting has become a more viable and financially prudent option than purchasing a home.

However, the preference for renting over homeownership is not solely a matter of financial necessity. Many renters, including families, young professionals, and empty nesters, are seeking more than just affordable housing. They desire a sense of community and a place that feels like home, with access to quality education, convenient shopping, and minimal commute times. They envision a lifestyle that includes a backyard for family gatherings, the joy of pet ownership, and the assurance of residing in a neighborhood where people care about their surroundings. These aspirations are increasingly attainable through the BTR model, which offers the amenities and lifestyle benefits traditionally associated with homeownership, but with the flexibility and affordability of renting.

The BTR model is not a threat to the American dream; rather, it is an evolution of that dream, adapting to the preferences and financial realities of modern living. By offering high-quality, community-oriented rental options, BTR developments are redefining what it means to have a place that feels like home, without the financial burden and permanence of homeownership. This shift represents a significant transformation in the way we perceive and pursue the ideal living situation, indicating that for a growing number of Americans, the dream of a perfect home can indeed be realized through renting.

As we explore the nuances of the BTR model and its implications for the future of housing, it's essential to recognize that this trend is not a departure from the American dream but a reflection of its evolving nature. The BTR model offers a pragmatic and desirable alternative for those who value the benefits of community, convenience, and affordability, signaling a broader transformation in the housing landscape that caters to the diverse needs and aspirations of today's households.

That's what BTR gives them.

BTR developments are reshaping the housing industry by merging the best attributes of SFRs with the enhanced living experience of a professionally managed community. This innovative approach to housing creates environments that are not just about providing a place to live but about fostering a sense of community and belonging. By situating all homes within gated, amenity-rich neighborhoods—complete with swimming pools, tennis courts, dog parks, and more—BTR developments offer a lifestyle that traditional homeownership or SFRs might not provide, all without the financial encumbrances of HOA fees or mortgage debt.

The significance of this trend extends far beyond the potential lifestyle benefits for residents. It represents a pivotal shift in the real estate sector that builders, investors, brokers, developers, realtors, and anyone with an interest in real estate investing should be aware of. The drive toward BTR is a multifaceted phenomenon, influenced by several key factors in the global economic landscape.

Firstly, the search for high-yield investments has become increasingly challenging against the backdrop of the pandemic-induced recession, rampant inflation, and prolonged economic uncertainties. These factors have driven bond yields to historic lows, compelling large funds to explore alternative avenues for returns. Secondly, traditional bastions of commercial real estate investment—such as office towers, retail centers, hotels, and apartments—have faced unprecedented challenges due to social distancing mandates and the widespread shift toward remote work. These sectors, once seen as reliable sources of income, have experienced significant disruptions, leading investors to seek more stable opportunities.

Single-family homes, by contrast, have demonstrated remarkable resilience throughout the pandemic. Despite the economic turbulence, the SFR segment has maintained healthy occupancy rates and consistent rent collection and has even witnessed rent increases. This stability has made SFRs, and by extension, BTR developments, highly attractive to investors looking for dependable returns. The allure of BTR is not just its potential to generate income but also its ability to adapt to changing lifestyles and preferences, offering a sustainable model for growth and investment in the real estate market.

As we delve deeper into the BTR model, it's clear that its rise is not merely a reaction to the current economic climate but a forward-looking adaptation to the evolving needs of modern residents and investors alike. BTR developments represent a confluence of economic viability, lifestyle preferences, and investment stability, positioning them as a significant and enduring trend in the real estate industry. This evolution underscores the need for stakeholders in the real estate sector to understand and engage with BTR, not just as a niche opportunity but as a transformative force reshaping the landscape of housing and investment.

Navigating the current real estate market presents a unique set of challenges, particularly for those aspiring to homeownership. The notion of purchasing a home under $200,000 has become increasingly elusive nationwide, with the average sales price in the US hovering around $350,000. This price point places the dream of owning a property beyond the financial reach of many, signaling a significant shift in the accessibility of homeownership for the average American.

The root causes of this shift are multifaceted, stemming from a combination of increased construction costs, significant labor shortages, and a general reluctance among major builders to embark on affordable housing projects. These factors contribute to a dwindling supply of newly built homes, exacerbating the already critical shortage in housing inventory. The resultant "hockey stick effect" on land values further complicates the picture, driving up costs at every stage of the home-buying process. This escalation in costs does not end with construction. Prospective homeowners must navigate the challenging terrain of property appraisals and mortgage qualification, adding additional layers of complexity to the home-buying process. These hurdles underscore a broader trend in the real estate market, where the barriers to homeownership are increasingly insurmountable for a large segment of the population.

The rapidity with which these changes have unfolded may seem startling, yet they are the culmination of trends that have been brewing for over two decades. This long-term shift reflects deeper structural changes in the economy, labor market, and the real estate industry itself. As we confront these challenges, the importance of innovative housing solutions such as the BTR model becomes ever more apparent. BTR offers a viable alternative to traditional homeownership, providing quality housing options that align with the financial realities and lifestyle preferences of many Americans.

In this context, the BTR model emerges not just as a response to current market dynamics but as a forward-thinking solution to a problem that has been decades in the making. By offering affordable, flexible, and community-oriented housing options, BTR developments represent a beacon of hope for those who find the dream of homeownership increasingly out of reach. As we look to the future, embracing and expanding the BTR model will be crucial in addressing the housing affordability crisis and ensuring that the dream of a home remains within reach for all.

The Origins of BTR

The origins of the BTR movement can be traced back to a pivotal moment in recent history—the 2008 housing industry collapse. This period marked a profound transformation in the landscape of single-family home rentals, catalyzed by the convergence of a global financial crisis and the resultant flood of foreclosures across the US. The crisis, precipitated by a wave of poorly underwritten mortgages, left millions of Americans facing the loss of their homes, setting the stage for a dramatic shift in the real estate market.

In the aftermath of the collapse, a new breed of investors emerged. Armed with substantial capital, these investors descended on foreclosure auctions, seizing the opportunity to acquire properties at significantly reduced prices. This phenomenon represented a departure from the traditional model of single-family home rentals, which had historically been dominated by small-scale, mom-and-pop investors. Instead, the market began to attract institutional investors and funds of a scale previously unseen in the realm of single-family homes.

This influx of large-scale investment capital into SFRs laid the groundwork for the evolution of the BTR sector. As institutional investors acquired properties en masse, they began to professionalize and institutionalize the management of single-family rental homes, treating them as a distinct asset class. This shift not only changed the dynamics of the rental market but also highlighted the potential for substantial returns on investment, drawing even more attention from large funds and investors. As we delve deeper into the origins and implications of the BTR movement, it becomes clear that this evolution is not just about real estate—it's about reimagining the very concept of home and community in the twenty-first century.

In the nascent stages following the 2008 financial crisis, the landscape of institutional investment in single-family homes was markedly sparse, with only a handful of players recognizing the untapped potential of this sector. However, the entry of Wall Street into the arena marked a seismic shift, as institutional investors began to acquire properties on a scale previously unimaginable. This influx of capital and interest transformed the SFR market, setting off a series of innovations and strategic recalibrations within the industry.

Initially, the strategy and long-term vision for these vast portfolios of single-family homes were not fully defined. Investors knew there was value to be extracted from these assets, but the optimal approach for capitalizing on their investments was still taking shape. Over time, it became apparent that leasing these homes, rather than flipping them postrenovation, offered a more sustainable and profitable model. This realization heralded a significant shift in strategy, moving away from the traditional buy-fix-sell model toward a buy-and-hold approach focused on generating steady rental income. Today, the market for SFR homes has matured significantly, with large portfolios being bought and sold in transactions that often bypass public listing services like Multiple Listing Service (MLS). Furthermore, the securitization of rent rolls and the inclusion of rental properties in real estate investment trusts (REITs) have elevated SFRs to a level of financial sophistication and public visibility that was previously unthinkable. These developments have not only legitimized SFRs as a viable investment class but have also facilitated greater liquidity, transparency, and access for investors ranging from individuals to large institutions.

The transformative impact of technology on the SFR market has been profound, reshaping the economics of property management and investment returns. The advent of advanced technologies, including artificial intelligence (AI) and specialized software programs, has revolutionized the way institutional investors manage their vast portfolios of rental properties. These technological innovations have enabled investors to streamline operations, significantly reducing the costs associated with property management. Traditionally, the management of rental properties was a labor-intensive process, often necessitating the involvement of property management companies that would charge approximately 10 percent of a property's overall income for their services. This model, while effective, posed a substantial overhead for investors, impacting the overall profitability of their rental portfolios. However, the introduction of sophisticated technology programs designed for the real estate sector has dramatically altered this landscape.

As we look to the future, the continued evolution of technology in the real estate sector promises further enhancements to the way properties are managed, rented, and sold. For institutional investors and hedge funds, these advancements represent a critical component of their strategy, enabling them to maintain competitive returns in a rapidly changing market. The intersection of real estate and technology continues to offer new opportunities for innovation, efficiency, and growth, marking a new era in the history of property investment.

The proliferation of advertisements offering to buy houses for cash is a testament to this shift. Where once "We Buy Ugly Houses" dominated the landscape with its omnipresent billboards, the digital age has ushered in a multitude of companies vying for a piece of the real estate investment pie. This change is largely facilitated by the power of social media and online marketing, which have democratized access to the real estate market, enabling a wider array of entities to participate in property investment. The rise of cash-for-houses advertisements is both a symbol and a driver of this change, reflecting the growing diversity of participants in the real estate market and the evolving strategies they employ. As the market continues to evolve, it is likely that we will see further democratization of real estate investment, enabled by technology and fueled by the entrepreneurial spirit of a new generation of investors.

Recognizing the significance of efficient and effective property management, these investors have moved toward vertical integration by establishing their own property management companies. This shift allows them to internalize the property management function, thereby optimizing operational efficiencies, reducing costs, and enhancing control over their investment portfolios. This move toward self-management represents a significant pivot in the strategy of institutional investors. Traditionally, the management of large portfolios of rental properties was outsourced to third-party property management firms. While effective, this approach introduced additional costs and sometimes resulted in a disconnect between the property owners' strategic objectives and the day-to-day operational execution by external managers. By forming their own property management entities, institutional investors are essentially "paying themselves" to manage their portfolios, ensuring that the operational aspects of property management are fully aligned with their broader investment strategies.

Who Are These Renters, and Why?

The demographics and motivations of renters in today's real estate market are reflective of broader societal shifts and changing perceptions of the American dream. The traditional view of homeownership as the quintessential goal is evolving, giving way to a more dynamic interpretation that values flexibility, mobility, and the freedom to experience new environments. This transformation is driven by several key factors, each contributing to the increasing preference for renting over owning.

Here are some of the reasons people choose renting over ownership:

More mobility: Modern lifestyles and work arrangements increasingly prioritize the ability to move freely and without the burdens associated with homeownership. For many, the appeal of being able to relocate for job opportunities, for personal growth, or simply for a change of scenery is a significant factor in choosing to rent. This mobility is especially valued by younger generations, such as millennials and Gen Z, who often seek varied experiences and do not necessarily view homeownership as a prerequisite for success or happiness.

Been there, done that: Many empty nesters from the boomer generation also prefer renting over homeownership these days. They enjoyed their homes while raising a family, but in retirement, they no longer want the responsibility of upkeep and, like younger generations, are looking for more mobility in their later years.

Work-from-anywhere culture: The proliferation of remote work, accelerated by the COVID-19 pandemic, has decoupled the traditional ties between one's job and their physical location. With a reliable internet connection, individuals can perform their roles from virtually anywhere, rendering the need to live in a specific location less critical. This flexibility has empowered more people to explore living situations that best suit their lifestyle preferences, rather than being anchored by the constraints of a mortgage or a specific job location.

No worries about the sales process: As a renter, there are no concerns about all the hassles of going through the purchase or sale of a house.

Economic considerations: The economic realities facing many individuals today also play a significant role in the shift toward renting. The rising costs of homeownership, including mortgage payments, property taxes, maintenance, and repairs, can be prohibitive for many, particularly in high-demand urban areas. Renting, on the other hand, offers a more predictable and often more affordable living arrangement, without the long-term financial commitment and liabilities associated with owning a home.

Not enough inventory: Currently, there just aren't enough freestanding houses to go around. So low inventory is leading many people to rent.

All these factors and more have contributed to an increase in hedge fund investments in American properties. In fact, hedge funds acquired 18 percent of every single-family home sold in the US in the third quarter of 2021, some $64 billion worth of properties.[1] During the first three months of 2023, that number increased to 27 percent of single-family homes.[2]

1   Lily Katz and Sheharyar Bokhari, "Real-Estate Investors Bought a Record 18% of the U.S. Homes That Sold in the Third Quarter," *Redfin News*, updated April 6, 2022, accessed February 2, 2024, https://www.redfin.com/news/investor-home-purchases-q3-2021/.

2   Christine Stuart, "Democratic Legislation Aims to Curb Hedge Fund Ownership of Single-Family Homes," *National Mortgage Professional*, December 8, 2023, accessed February 2, 2024, https://nationalmortgageprofessional.com/news/democratic-legislation-aims-curb-hedge-fund-ownership-single-family-homes.

Reshaping the Rules

The presence of institutional investors in the single-family home market, holding 27 percent of all homes in the US, is significantly altering the dynamics of real estate transactions, ownership patterns, and market expectations. This shift not only impacts the availability and pricing of homes but also has broader implications for first-time homebuyers, individual sellers, and the real estate profession at large.

For instance, first-time homebuyers, often reliant on mortgage financing, find themselves at a significant disadvantage when competing against cash offers from institutional investors. The ability of these investors to close deals quickly and without financing contingencies makes them more attractive to sellers, especially in a competitive market. This dynamic can limit access to affordable housing for first-time buyers, who are a crucial demographic in sustaining healthy homeownership rates and community stability. With a considerable portion of the market under the control of institutional investors, the landscape of resale inventory, particularly in the sub-$300,000 category, is changing. Homes in this price range are increasingly likely to be sold by institutions rather than individuals, altering the traditional homeowner-to-homeowner transaction model. This shift could lead to changes in how homes are priced, marketed, and sold, potentially streamlining processes but also introducing new challenges for individual buyers and sellers.

The increasing dominance of institutional investors could also impact the traditional real estate commission model. Institutions, with their vast portfolios and streamlined operations, may opt for alternative selling strategies that bypass traditional listing services and agent representation. This could lead to reduced commission rates or the adoption of fixed-fee services, affecting the income of real estate professionals and potentially altering the landscape of the real estate brokerage industry. Real estate professionals will need to innovate their services and value propositions to remain relevant and competitive.

For buyers, especially first-timers, understanding the market dynamics and exploring creative financing or purchase strategies becomes even more critical. The growing role of institutional investors in the housing market may also prompt considerations for policy and regulation aimed at ensuring fair access to housing, maintaining affordable housing stock, and preserving the interests of individual homeowners and communities. As the market continues to evolve, the challenge for policymakers, industry professionals, and market participants will be to balance the efficiency and capital that institutional investors bring with the needs and aspirations of individual homeowners and communities.

The shifting dynamics of the real estate market, driven in part by the increasing presence of institutional investors, present both challenges and opportunities for traditional real estate agents. The conventional model of selling homes—one property at a time, primarily to individual buyers and sellers—may not align with the future landscape of real estate transactions. These changes necessitate a strategic reevaluation of how agents operate, highlighting the need for adaptation and innovation in their approaches to remain relevant and successful. For clients, the evolving market may necessitate more comprehensive advisory services from agents, including guidance on navigating competitive buying situations, understanding new selling strategies, and considering alternative housing options or investment strategies. However, the increasing role of institutional investors in the real estate market does not spell the end of the road for traditional agents. Instead, it underscores the importance of adaptability, lifelong learning, and innovation in sustaining and growing their careers amid changing market conditions. Agents who proactively embrace these changes, refine their strategies, and continuously seek to add value for their clients can navigate the evolving landscape successfully and maintain their relevance in the industry.

The saturation of agents relative to the available inventory of active properties also presents a unique set of challenges for traditional real estate agents. This imbalance—exacerbated by the previously mentioned entrance of hedge funds and institutional investors into the market—further intensifies competition and complicates the dynamics of buying and selling homes, especially in the affordable housing segment. With 90 percent of agents operating in the affordable housing space, the oversaturation in this segment leads to heightened competition among agents. This focus on affordable housing is driven by the high demand among first-time buyers, but the shrinking inventory due to institutional purchases limits opportunities for agents and buyers alike. Becoming an expert in a particular area of real estate, such as luxury properties, historic homes, or specific neighborhoods, can help agents differentiate themselves. While the luxury market is smaller, it's less saturated with agents and less affected by institutional buying trends. As the real estate market continues to evolve, agents who redefine their roles by adapting their strategies, embracing new opportunities, and focusing on adding value for their clients will be better positioned to thrive and succeed amid changing conditions.

The evolving dynamics of the real estate market also includes a shift toward nonnegotiable pricing strategies by institutional owners and an increasing availability of technology-driven real estate services. Combined, these further call into question the value proposition of traditional agents in the buying and selling process, which has often been closely tied to their ability to negotiate deals on behalf of their clients. With institutional investors setting firm prices and refusing to negotiate, the agent's role in securing favorable terms for their clients is significantly reduced. Platforms like Opendoor and Offerpad offer streamlined, technology-driven processes for buying and selling homes, further diminishing the need for traditional real estate agents. These platforms often provide fixed pricing models and simplified transaction processes, appealing to buyers and sellers seeking convenience and efficiency. The lack of negotiation in transactions with institutional sellers limits the control real estate agents have over the buying or selling experience. This shift reduces the agent's ability to influence outcomes, potentially making their involvement seem less necessary to clients.

However, the story of helping a first-time buyer, particularly one who is an immigrant to the US, to purchase their first home illustrates the unique value that real estate agents have traditionally brought to the table. Beyond the mere facilitation of a transaction, agents have played a key role in guiding, educating, and supporting their clients through one of the most significant decisions of their lives. This process often involves building a deep understanding of the client's needs, fears, aspirations, and dreams, fostering a connection that transcends the transaction itself. As the industry shifts toward a more institutionalized model, with a potential reduction in commission percentages, agents are confronted with the challenge of reassessing how they add value to their clients and sustain their livelihoods. The standard commission of 3 percent on a sale, already a subject of debate and variation across the industry, could face further pressure, particularly if agents are perceived as adding less value in a market dominated by large-scale investors and digital platforms. The shift from relationship-based to transactional contracts in real estate reflects broader changes in society and the economy. Yet it also reaffirms the inherent value of personal connections, trust, and understanding in the home-buying and selling process.

For real estate agents committed to their profession, the challenge is to navigate these changes without losing the essence of what makes their work meaningful: the ability to make a profound impact on their clients' lives. By reimagining their roles and embracing both the emotional and practical aspects of real estate, agents can continue to thrive in an industry that is, at its heart, about helping people find their place in the world.

The Shift from SFR to BTR

The genesis of the BTR phenomenon by the influx of institutional investors armed with substantial capital earmarked for property acquisitions created intense competition that led to a natural compression of yields as investors vied for the same properties, often through the nationwide MLS, driving up prices and diminishing the potential returns on investment. This pressure to find untapped opportunities in a crowded market catalyzed the innovative leap toward BTR developments by investors who saw the potential in the BTR model amid diminishing returns and increasing difficulty of acquiring existing SFR assets. By stepping outside the confines of the conventional acquisition model, investors not only found a solution to the challenges of a competitive and saturated market but also tapped into a growing demand for rental housing that offers the flexibility, amenities, and lifestyle that modern renters seek.

Before the rise of BTR developments, institutional investors engaging in the SFR market faced a myriad of challenges, particularly related to the acquisition, renovation, and management of older homes. The traditional process involved purchasing individual properties—often homes built decades ago—and undertaking significant renovations to update and repair them to meet rental market standards. This model, while potentially lucrative, came with its own set of complexities and inefficiencies. Investors often targeted homes with a desirable basic structure, such as a three-bedroom, two-bath house, but these properties frequently required extensive updates. Renovations could range from cosmetic improvements, like replacing outdated light fixtures and painting, to more substantial overhauls involving plumbing, electrical systems, and HVAC. The goal was to modernize the home, making it appealing to renters and minimizing the need for ongoing maintenance. However, the reality of renovating older properties often meant dealing with unexpected issues—hidden damages, code compliance, and delays in obtaining parts or labor.

For institutional investors and individual landlords alike, maintaining a stable and attractive cap rate is crucial for the financial viability of their real estate investments. The capitalization rate, or cap rate, is a fundamental metric used in the real estate industry to estimate the return on investment (ROI) for a property. It's calculated by dividing the property's annual net operating income (NOI) by its current market value or purchase price. The distinction between investing in older, renovated homes versus newly constructed properties in the BTR sector significantly impacts the stability and predictability of these cap rates. Investing in older homes and renovating them for rental purposes introduces a level of financial uncertainty, primarily due to fluctuating repair and maintenance costs. Significant components like air conditioning, roofing, HVAC, and plumbing can incur substantial expenses, affecting the property's NOI and, consequently, its cap rate. Older properties are more susceptible to wear and tear, leading to unpredictable maintenance needs that can arise unexpectedly and require immediate attention, disrupting the financial stability of the investment.

Conversely, new construction comes with warranties covering major components and systems, such as HVAC, roofing, and plumbing. These warranties protect the investor from significant repair costs, at least during the warranty period, providing a buffer against unexpected financial outlays. By design, new constructions have minimal immediate maintenance needs. This not only reduces short-term maintenance costs but also allows for a more predictable financial model, because the likelihood of unforeseen repairs is significantly lower compared to older properties. Any initial defects or issues that arise shortly after construction are typically the responsibility of the builder or developer to correct. This arrangement further insulates the investor from early-stage repair costs, enhancing the investment's financial stability. The shift toward BTR developments reflects a strategic response to the challenges of managing older rental properties, offering a compelling case for the stability and financial predictability that new constructions can provide to investors in the real estate market.

The rapid expansion of BTR communities, with a growth rate around 10 percent over just five years, underscores a significant transformation within the real estate landscape. This surge in development reflects the BTR sector's response to a wide array of housing needs, positioning it as a pivotal solution in the pursuit of affordable, quality housing. The appeal of BTR communities lies in their ability to cater to a diverse demographic, offering a variety of housing options that reflect the varied lifestyles and needs of modern residents. BTR developments are designed with community at their core, fostering a sense of belonging and connectivity among residents. Unlike traditional rental options, BTR communities are planned and built with the intention of creating a neighborhood feel, offering shared amenities such as parks, recreational facilities, community centers, and sometimes even retail and dining options. This emphasis on community-building enhances the quality of life for residents, making BTR neighborhoods not just places to live, but places where people are genuinely happy to come home. The success of BTR communities lies in their ability to merge the practical benefits of rental living with the emotional and social needs of a home, creating environments where people from diverse backgrounds and life stages can find a place to call home. As this segment continues to grow, it represents a transformative force in the real estate market, reshaping perceptions of rental living and providing a blueprint for the future of housing development.

REMEMBER:

- → Build-to-rent (BTR) is a new kind of rental community.
- → These are not one-size-fits-all.
- → More people from many walks of life are renting these days.
- → A shortage of affordable housing, high costs to build, and a flood of institutional investors are all making it tougher to be a homeowner.
- → BTR is a viable option for affordable housing.
- → Realtors must pivot to maintain their value for the consumer.
- → The American dream of homeownership is evolving.
- → BTR is here, and it's not going away.

CHAPTER 2

HOW IT WORKS

The narrative of the early days of real estate investment is a compelling one, marked by a hands-on approach to property evaluation and the inherent challenges of dealing with distressed properties. In this chapter, I'll delve into the transformative journey of the real estate investment landscape, particularly through the lens of early experiences navigating the market's opportunities and the personal resilience, adaptability, and expertise developed through navigating the market's challenges. It's a vivid portrayal of the shift from a buy/flip model to a strategic focus on rental properties as a source of cap rate return, a transition significantly influenced by Wall Street's entry into the market.

In 2009, the real estate investment strategy primarily revolved around purchasing distressed properties to flip for a profit. This approach, however, began to evolve as institutional investors recognized the potential for generating steady returns through renting these properties. This paradigm shift was not instantaneous but marked by gradual recognition of the long-term value and stability offered by rental income, contrasting with the quick, often speculative gains of flipping properties.

The nascent stage of investment real estate was fraught with challenges, notably the absence of technology platforms for quick underwriting, ARV (After Repair Value) valuations, or cap rate calculations. This lack of technological support necessitated a hands-on, sometimes perilous approach to property evaluation, leading to encounters with squatters, dangerous animals, and hazardous living conditions—I personally experienced many of these precarious situations firsthand when previewing properties for investors early in my career. These experiences underscore the gritty reality of real estate investment, far removed from its perceived glamour. Navigating the challenges of early real estate investment not only required resilience and adaptability but also contributed significantly to personal growth and the development of expertise in the sector. The experiences of dealing with unexpected and sometimes dangerous situations served as a crucible, forging a deep understanding of the market's complexities and the skills necessary to succeed.

Then 2015 marked a pivotal moment in our journey within the real estate investment sector. This period underscored the remarkable evolution from the early, hands-on days of navigating property investments to leveraging advanced technology and strategic approaches that significantly enhanced our operational efficiency and investment outcomes. The transition to working with our first institutional client represented not just a scale of operations previously unimaginable but also a testament to how technology reshaped the landscape of real estate investing.

At the time, the adoption of investment software and sophisticated cap rate calculations enabled our team to undertake a groundbreaking approach to property acquisitions. We were sending offers sight unseen, a strategy that hinged on the reliability and precision of our technological tools. This method allowed us to evaluate properties, estimate potential returns, and make informed decisions with a speed and accuracy that traditional methods could never match.

The success of closing over five hundred homes in just ten months was not solely due to technology but also to the streamlined structure of our real estate team. Comprising five to six agents and a transaction manager, our team was a well-oiled machine, capable of handling the sheer volume of transactions that our institutional client required. This efficiency was a direct result of not only the dedication and skill of our team members but also the integrative power of technology, which facilitated communication, documentation, and coordination across numerous transactions.

The transition from hands-on property scouting to managing hundreds of transactions through technological means within a span of just a few years illustrates the dynamic nature of the real estate investment sector. It highlights the importance of adaptability, the willingness to embrace new technologies, and the need for a cohesive and highly efficient team. This chapter of our experience not only showcases our growth and success but also mirrors the broader shifts in the industry toward greater reliance on technology to drive investment strategies and operational efficiencies.

Institutional capital has significantly transformed the residential real estate market by introducing sophisticated investment strategies that leverage Wall Street capital. This transformation is underpinned by the development of advanced algorithms that utilize extensive real estate rental data. These algorithms calculate potential returns on investment, enabling institutional investors to identify and acquire residential properties nationwide, thereby offering attractive returns to their shareholders. This strategic approach not only capitalizes on the residential sector's potential but also skillfully mitigates the risks typically associated with real estate development.

The entry of institutional capital into the residential real estate market, guided by sophisticated algorithms and strategic data analysis, represents a notable shift in investment paradigms. This approach not only offers an innovative avenue for deploying Wall Street capital but also highlights the evolving nature of real estate as an investment class. As rents continue to rise and the residential market remains robust, this strategy underscores the growing intersection between technology, finance, and real estate, promising consistent and attractive returns for investors while minimizing traditional development risks.

The advent of institutional funds building entire BTR communities represents a significant evolution in the real estate investment landscape. These developments are tailored to meet the increasing demand for rental properties that offer an affordable lifestyle without compromising on quality or amenities.

The strategic shift toward creating such communities not only addresses a crucial market need but also heralds a new era of investment opportunities that promise substantial returns and the opportunity to meet the housing needs of a diverse population. As this segment continues to grow, it will likely become a cornerstone of the investment landscape, provided that developers and investors navigate market dynamics, regulatory environments, and community integration effectively. The success of BTR developments hinges on their ability to offer value to both investors and residents, making them a critical component of the future of housing.

The strategic decision-making process behind where to develop BTR communities is complex and multifaceted, requiring a thorough analysis of various factors that influence potential returns and market viability. BTR operators meticulously evaluate a range of elements to identify locations that not only promise high cap rate returns but also align with the lifestyle preferences and needs of potential tenants. Understanding these considerations is crucial for developers aiming to capitalize on the burgeoning BTR market while mitigating risks associated with new developments.

The process of identifying suitable locations for BTR developments involves a delicate balance of analyzing hard data on rental rates and demographics with softer considerations like community and lifestyle fit. The ultimate question of whether the opportunity outweighs the risk is central to the strategic planning of BTR operators. Successfully navigating this complex landscape requires not only a deep understanding of market dynamics but also a nuanced appreciation of the evolving needs and preferences of renters.

Types of Properties

The BTR sector encompasses a variety of property types designed to cater to different market segments and demographic areas. The strategic approach to developing these properties involves careful consideration of market demands, rental rates, and the broader goal of enhancing the value of the surrounding area.

Here's an overview of the dynamics that shape the types of properties within the BTR space and the operational strategies that ensure their success and sustainability.

BTR homes can vary significantly in price, typically ranging from $175,000 to $400,000, reflecting the diversity of locations and target demographics they aim to serve. Whether aimed at young professionals, families, or empty nesters, the development of BTR communities is guided by a thorough understanding of the current market.

This includes analyzing demographic trends, income levels, and local housing demand to produce a product that not only meets the needs of potential tenants but also adds value to the community.

A critical component of the BTR model is the reliance on professional property management companies with a proven track record of managing assets for institutional investors. These companies play a pivotal role in maintaining the high standards of BTR communities, from the screening of tenants to ensure the selection of responsible and reliable occupants, to the ongoing maintenance and repair of properties. This professional oversight is fundamental to preserving the quality and appeal of BTR communities.

Contrary to the misconception that rental communities are more prone to deterioration, BTR operators and their property management partners place a strong emphasis on regular maintenance and timely repairs. This proactive approach to property upkeep is essential for sustaining the quality of individual homes and communal amenities, thereby ensuring that BTR communities remain attractive and competitive in the rental market.

As a new paradigm in housing, BTR offers a range of properties that respond to the diverse needs and preferences of today's renters. Through strategic development, rigorous tenant screening, and professional property management, BTR operators are able to provide high-quality living spaces that challenge the traditional views of rental communities. The success of these communities hinges on a multifaceted approach that prioritizes market alignment, property upkeep, and community engagement, ensuring that BTR developments remain a vibrant and valuable part of the housing landscape.

Features of BTR Single-Family Homes

BTR single-family homes offer a distinctive living experience that merges the benefits of traditional homeownership with the flexibility and convenience of renting. These communities, typically ranging from thirty to two hundred homes per development, are meticulously designed to cater to the modern renter's needs, offering a plethora of features that set them apart from conventional apartment living in urban centers.

Here's an overview of the key features that define BTR single-family homes: Our traditional unit count for all of our current BTR communities normally averages from seventy units to two hundred units depending on location, and any restrictions. The features of BTR single-family homes provide a compelling alternative to both traditional homeownership and apartment living. By offering the privacy, space, and amenities desired by modern renters, along with the flexibility and ease of a rental arrangement, BTR communities are setting a new standard in residential living. As the demand for affordable, high-quality rental options continues to grow, BTR single-family homes are well-positioned to meet this need, reshaping the landscape of the rental market. BTR homes are built with the modern renter in mind, featuring high-quality construction and contemporary finishes. Developers often equip these homes with modern appliances, energy-efficient systems, and high-speed internet access, ensuring a comfortable and convenient lifestyle for tenants.

BTR developments are innovating the rental market by incorporating diverse housing formats and eco-friendly features, which not only cater to a broader range of tenant preferences but also command higher rents due to their unique offerings. This innovative approach not only enhances the living experience for renters but also presents developers with the opportunity to differentiate their properties in a competitive market. The inclusion of townhomes, duplexes, and zero-energy homes in these communities speaks to the evolving demands of renters who seek sustainability, convenience, and a sense of community in their living spaces.

By integrating various types of homes, such as townhomes and duplexes, BTR developments offer choices that appeal to different demographics. This variety enables tenants to select a home that best fits their lifestyle, whether they're looking for the compact efficiency of a duplex or the spacious layout of a townhome.

The integration of smart home technology in BTR properties caters to tenants who value convenience and efficiency. Features such as smart thermostats, energy-efficient appliances, and home automation systems enhance the living experience by providing comfort, security, and energy savings. Amenities like clubhouses, gyms, pools, and sports courts add value to BTR communities by promoting a lifestyle that extends beyond the walls of the home. These facilities not only serve as hubs for social interaction and physical activity but also contribute to the overall attractiveness of the development. As the BTR sector continues to evolve, its ability to adapt to niche demands and sustainability trends will likely play a key role in its growth and success.

In Texas where I operate, my team and I focus on single-family properties. These are the homes that tend to fill most quickly and are most in need, so for the purposes of discussion in this book, that's what I will focus on.

While there are some standard configurations and features, each home is different, outside and inside. The homes, generally spanning from 1,600 to 2,200 square feet, are designed to cater to a wide range of lifestyles, offering both standard and customizable features that enhance the living experience. The size range of these homes is strategically chosen to appeal to various household types, from smaller families and couples to individuals seeking more space than typically offered in urban apartment settings. This range provides ample room for comfortable living, work-from-home setups, and entertainment without the maintenance challenges of larger properties.

On the outside, each home has a different type of façade and siding. Later in the book I'll discuss exit strategies, but for now, know that these communities are built with the exit strategy in mind and if that strategy is to ultimately sell off the homes to individual home owners after there has been a sufficient return on investment, then it's important for them to look different on the outside.

Inside, there are different layouts and styles, so they are not identical to each other. Depending on the development, configurations include three or four bedrooms, one or two baths, and a one- or two-car garage. In addition to bedrooms and baths, floor plans include a living room, dining room, open kitchen, laundry room, and walk-in closets. These two-story homes range from 1,600 to 2,200 square feet, and every home has a front yard and a backyard and allows pets.

Internal features designed to minimize risks of damage include laminate flooring and granite or marble countertops in the kitchen and master bath, all in a limited number of colors to allow for bulk buying and to shave off some of the costs of construction. However, these are not custom-built homes where the consumer is given a selection of choices; interior materials are chosen by the developer.

Most single-family BTR communities include as few extra amenities as possible to prevent dealing with deferred maintenance or liabilities that come with features such as a pool, or clubhouse, or gym. Any BTR really needs about one hundred homes to really be able to utilize those types of amenities, otherwise the additional costs of maintaining these features negate the ability to keep the rent in the affordable range.

Instead, many BTR communities have a simple water feature surrounded by a walking path. But these water features actually have a purpose: they are detention ponds designed to capture stormwater runoff. Some also include a dog park feature but pet restrictions are similar to any rental property development—no dangerous dog breeds, for instance.

Most BTR properties also feature traditional wood fencing, unless there is a water feature, in which case fencing along the side facing the feature may be composed of wrought iron.

Restrictions and Responsibilities

In BTR communities, restrictions and responsibilities are established by the institutional investor and developer in accordance with their objectives and standards. These guidelines are designed to uphold the quality, integrity, and value of the community while ensuring a positive living experience for residents.

Here's how restrictions and responsibilities are typically managed in BTR communities: Institutional investors play a significant role in setting the framework for restrictions and responsibilities within BTR communities. Their primary goal is to safeguard their investment and maximize returns by maintaining the property's appeal and value over time. As such, they often implement stringent guidelines to govern various aspects of community living, from property maintenance to tenant behavior. Developers work closely with institutional investors to establish restrictions and responsibilities that align with the project's vision and goals. They bring expertise in community planning, design, and construction to ensure that the implemented guidelines contribute to the overall success of the development. Developers may also be responsible for enforcing these restrictions during the initial stages of community establishment.

Many BTR communities are managed by property management companies selected or affiliated with the institutional investor. These management entities are entrusted with overseeing day-to-day operations, enforcing community rules, and addressing tenant concerns. Their involvement ensures consistent implementation of restrictions and responsibilities while providing residents with reliable support and assistance.

Renters in BTR communities are often tasked with maintaining the backyard of their rented property. Guidelines are provided outlining acceptable practices and restrictions to ensure consistency and aesthetics across the community. This empowers tenants to personalize their outdoor space while also fostering a sense of ownership and pride in their living environment.

Conversely, the front yard is typically cared for by the property management company or maintenance staff employed by the investor or developer. This ensures that the frontage of each property maintains a uniform and well-maintained appearance, contributing to the overall curb appeal of the community. Property management teams handle tasks such as lawn mowing, landscaping, and exterior upkeep to uphold visual standards and property values. Effective communication between tenants, property management, and investors is essential to ensure that maintenance responsibilities are clearly understood and upheld. Regular communication channels, such as community newsletters, tenant portals, and onsite management, facilitate transparency and cooperation among all stakeholders.

In BTR communities, similar to traditional homeowners' associations (HOAs), there are specific restrictions and guidelines in place to maintain the integrity, aesthetics, and functionality of the neighborhood. These restrictions are established to promote a cohesive living environment and uphold property values. Renters are typically prohibited from operating a business within the residence. This restriction helps preserve the residential character of the community and prevents commercial activities from disrupting the neighborhood. There are restrictions on the number of cars that can be parked outside the house to prevent overcrowding and maintain adequate street access. Additionally, limitations may be imposed on the parking of campers, boats, or other recreational vehicles to ensure orderly parking and prevent obstruction of streets and driveways. Guidelines govern the construction of additional structures in the backyard, such as small storage units or sheds. However, there may be restrictions on the size, type, and placement of these structures to maintain uniformity and prevent visual clutter. For example, metal buildings taller than the house may be prohibited to preserve the overall aesthetic of the community. BTR communities often have regulations in place to address noise disturbances and nuisances that may disrupt the peace and quiet of the neighborhood. These regulations help promote a peaceful and harmonious living environment for all residents.

In BTR communities, where tenants typically reside for an average of three to five years, some renters may opt to undertake remodeling or repainting projects during their stay to personalize their living space. However, to uphold the uniformity and aesthetics of the neighborhood, there are often restrictions on paint colors for any repainting done inside or outside the property. Tenants are usually provided with a preapproved palette or a list of acceptable paint colors for interior repainting projects. These color options are carefully curated to maintain consistency and harmony throughout the community. Renters are encouraged to choose from these

approved colors to ensure that their interior modifications comple-
ment the overall aesthetic of the neighborhood. Property management
companies or homeowner associations responsible for overseeing
BTR communities typically enforce these restrictions on paint colors
through a compliance monitoring process. Tenants are informed of
the guidelines and are expected to comply with the established regulations. Noncompliance may result in corrective actions or penalties to
ensure adherence to community standards.

The question often arises about HOA fees, since these are new
developments. Whether there is an actual HOA fee involved comes
down to whether the development is in a Municipal Utility District
(MUD) or a Public Improvement District (PID). These districts
dictate some of the restrictions that are placed on the properties
within their boundaries. When a MUD or PID is in place, HOA fees
are required for BTR homes within their boundaries. The details of
MUDs and PIDs can be somewhat complicated, but let me share a
simplified explanation of what these are about.

MUDs and PIDs are unique to Texas. A MUD is a district
created by the State of Texas as authorized by the Texas Commission of Environmental Quality (TCEQ). MUDs are designed to help
finance the new construction of public infrastructure, such as roads,
water and sewer utilities, and proper drainage. Developers working
within a MUD are reimbursed for the infrastructure they install as
incentive and financial assistance for creating new neighborhoods.
Owners of the homes within the MUD are billed monthly for water
and sewer and are taxed annually in lieu of the city tax. These amounts
are assessed to the investment group as the owners of the properties,

which then includes those figures in the monthly rent charged for occupying the property in the form of an HOA.[3]

A PID (Public Improvement District) is similar to a MUD; however, improvements to sidewalks, landscaped areas, and parks or recreational facilities are also included as are features for public safety and security, parking areas, and other amenities. These improvements and maintenance are funded through bonds secured by liens against the property and based on the property's appraised value. The bonds are paid back by assessments to the property owners within the PID (the investment group), which again, are then included as part of the monthly HOA fee.[4]

The Difference Deferred Maintenance Makes

The absence of deferred maintenance in new BTR homes is a significant advantage for investors compared to older properties. Deferred maintenance refers to the backlog of necessary repairs and renovations that accumulate over time in a property. That's common for an investor who, for instance, buys a house built in 1980. A home that old is going to inevitably need some level of renovation before it can be rented, and there is always going to be deferred maintenance. Even when new plumbing is installed, something else will break and need repair. Roof, HVAC, plumbing, garbage disposals, structural repairs, foundation—the list goes on and on. The absence of deferred maintenance with BTRs simplifies property management for investors and their management teams. Instead of constantly addressing repair

---

3   "MUDs, PIDs, PUDs & TIFs: What REALTORS® Need To Know," *MetroTex Association of REALTORS*, accessed July 17, 2022, https://www.mymetrotex.com/muds-pids-puds-tifs-what-realtors-need-to-know.

4   Ibid.

requests and scheduling maintenance tasks, property managers can focus on providing excellent customer service and enhancing the overall tenant experience. This underscores the attractiveness of BTR investments as a low-maintenance, high-value proposition in the real estate market.

With new construction development, there is zero or very limited deferred maintenance for at least a three- to five-year period. That allows investors to achieve a return on their investment without the fluctuations of a traditional single-family portfolio. Deferred maintenance kills returns; if ten properties in a portfolio all need roofs, that could be a quarter-million-dollar expense. In a new community, out of ten properties, maybe one will have a faulty garbage disposal that needs to be replaced in three to five years, but few, if any, major elements will need a costly repair or replacement. New BTR homes are built to modern construction standards and often come with warranties for major components such as roofing, HVAC systems, and appliances. This helps preserve the property's value over the long term and minimizes the risk of depreciation associated with deferred maintenance in older properties.

When analyzing a single-family rental option for an investor, we typically look at rent multiplied by twelve minus any HOA fee and taxes, then divide that by the sales price. That gives us the capital expenditures rate (CapEx) or cap rate, which is how we look at getting a double-digit return. It's basically what to offer on a property, and then the overall price to pay minus the repairs off of the sales price.

Rent x 12 – HOA and taxes / sales price = cap rate

Figuring cap rate involves different algorithms and options, and no two investors use the same calculations. A simplified explanation is that, if the cap rate tells us that we can spend $250,000 on each home all-in, then we discover that a property needs $20,000 in repairs, the repair costs have to come off the asking price to secure the gross cap rate. A net cap rate or net return includes holding costs, insurance, and other fees that the investor needs to charge themselves.

Most institutional investors negotiate a warranty with the builder of BTR communities. This warranty covers defects or malfunctions in various components of the property, ranging from minor issues like faucet leaks to more significant concerns such as structural integrity, including roof leaks. The builder is responsible for addressing and rectifying these issues within the specified warranty period. While the builder warranties cover most issues within the property, tenants are expected to take responsibility for certain types of damage or incidents. For example, damage caused by the tenant's negligence, such as a clogged toilet, may not be covered under the builder warranty. Similarly, damage resulting from natural disasters like wind or hurricanes may fall outside the scope of the warranty. By implementing these warranties and insurance policies, institutional investors can minimize their exposure to risks associated with property ownership while providing tenants with peace of mind and protection against unforeseen events. These measures contribute to the overall safety, security, and sustainability of BTR communities in the real estate market.

BTR around the World

Indeed, BTR is a growing trend not limited to the US, with variations in structure and demand seen in different regions worldwide. Here's a glimpse of how BTR is evolving in various parts of the world.

In Sydney, BTR developments have gained momentum, driven partly by the influx of renters migrating from overseas, particularly from regions where apartment living is prevalent.[5] The demand for BTR properties in Sydney is fueled by factors such as lifestyle preferences, housing affordability challenges, and the desire for modern amenities and community living spaces. BTR has established a strong foothold in the UK's property market, with significant investment pouring into purpose-built rental housing across major cities like London, Manchester, and Birmingham. The UK government has actively supported BTR initiatives to address housing shortages and promote long-term rental options for residents. BTR developments in the UK often feature high-quality amenities, concierge services, and communal facilities tailored to urban lifestyles. Canadian cities like Toronto, Vancouver, and Montreal are witnessing a surge in BTR developments, driven by factors such as urbanization, population growth, and changing demographics. BTR projects in Canada cater to diverse tenant needs, offering a mix of rental options ranging from studio apartments to family-sized units. These developments emphasize sustainability, community engagement, and transit-oriented design to enhance livability and urban connectivity. BTR is gaining traction in various European cities, including Berlin, Amsterdam, and Stockholm, where housing affordability concerns and shifting lifestyle preferences are driving demand for purpose-built rental accommodation. European BTR projects often prioritize energy efficiency, green building standards, and innovative design concepts to align with sustainable urban development goals and promote tenant well-being.

Some areas of the world are more welcoming than others. While New South Wales, in Australia, is offering a land tax discount for

---

5   Shane Wright, "Sydney Residents Move Out as City Depends on Migrants for Growth," *Sydney Morning Herald,* March 27, 2019, accessed February 24, 2024, https://www.smh.com.au/politics/federal/sydney-residents-move-out-as-city-depends-on-migrants-for-growth-20190327-p5182y.html.

BTRs[6], New Zealand declined a tax exemption request by BTR investors. The request involved a rule that would have allowed interest on debt to be written off as an expense, but it was denied because owner-occupiers are not allowed to write off interest on their mortgages. The government denied the request in an effort to make investor-owned property less attractive, although a number of other incentives are in place as attempts to balance the need for new construction for private ownership with the need for additional properties to be used for rental purposes. One of the challenges is a resistance to classifying BTRs as a new asset class.[7]

So what exactly determines an ideal piece of land for a BTR community? That's what we'll look at in the next chapter.

---

6   Mirage.news, July 29, 202, https://www.miragenews.com/
      land-tax-cut-to-drive-build-to-rent-revolution/.

7   Jenée Tibshraeny, "Government Declines Request for 'Build-to-Rent' Developments
      to Be Exempt from the Interest Deduction Tax Change, but Continues to Consider
      Ways to Support the Sector," *interest.co.nz*, March 11, 2022, accessed February 24,
      2024, https://www.interest.co.nz/property/114768/government-declines-request-
      build-rent-developments-be-exempt-interest-deduction.

REMEMBER:

- ➡ Many types of properties are suited to the BTR model.

- ➡ In Texas, we focus on single-family homes, because those are most in demand.

- ➡ BTR homes have the same features and amenities as traditional homes: open floor plans, three or four bedrooms, one or two bathrooms, laundry room, and one- or two-car garage.

- ➡ BTR homes rent for around $2,000 per month but offer renters a more homelike space, with a front yard and a backyard.

- ➡ Property management by the investor group typically cares for the front yards of each property.

- ➡ Renters adhere to guidelines set by the investor group and developer.

- ➡ A plus for investors is that newly built BTRs are typically maintenance free for three to five years.

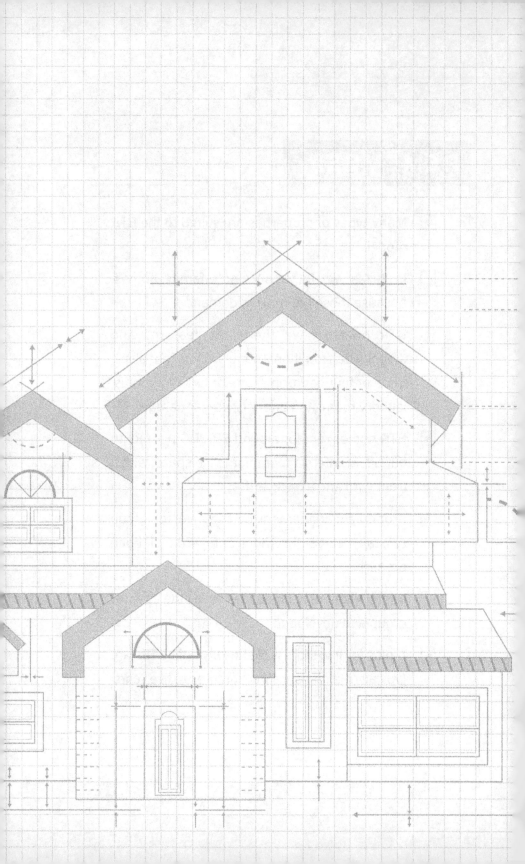

CHAPTER 3

FIRST STEPS TO IDENTIFY A VALID BUILD-TO-RENT SITE

When embarking on the journey of identifying a viable BTR land site, meticulous assessment and strategic evaluation become paramount. Here's an insight into the initial steps we undertake in our rigorous process.

We delve into comprehensive research to gauge the demand for rental properties, understanding the nuances of tenant preferences and rental trends in the area. This forms the bedrock of our decision-making process, guiding us toward areas with robust rental demand and growth potential. Next, we embark on a quest to uncover prime locations ripe for BTR development. We prioritize sites situated in close proximity to key amenities and conveniences, such as transportation hubs, employment centers, educational institutions, shopping districts, and recreational facilities. Accessibility and lifestyle appeal are pivotal factors guiding our site selection process. Understanding the competitive landscape is pivotal in shaping our strategy. We conduct a thorough analysis of existing rental properties in the vicinity, identifying market gaps and unmet tenant needs. By discerning the strengths and weaknesses of competitors, we glean valuable insights to position our BTR development for success. By meticulously navigating through these initial steps, we lay the foundation for identifying a promising build-to-rent site that not only meets market demands but also holds the potential for long-term success and profitability.

Thorough due diligence prior to making an offer on land for a BTR project can prevent unwanted problems from occurring. This chapter will cover all of the extensive analytics that go into selecting a location and will provide a step-by-step process to avoid missing any necessary steps when identifying a valid BTR site.

Absolutely, the landscape of real estate development has evolved significantly with the emergence of data-driven insights and specialized consulting firms. Companies like John Burns Research and Consulting and Yardi have played pivotal roles in equipping developers with valuable market intelligence, enabling informed decision-making and strategic planning.

Incorporating extensive due diligence is essential to ensure that a BTR community delivers the same level of value and lifestyle opportunities as traditional for-sale subdivisions. Here's a glimpse into the multifaceted due diligence process involved:

Location, Location, Location

Absolutely, location is paramount when it comes to build-to-rent properties, influencing rental income, tenant demand, and overall profitability. Selecting a prime location can significantly enhance the potential for profitability and ensure the long-term success of your development.

Build-to-rent communities are strategically situated within close proximity—typically within thirty-five to forty minutes—of major metropolitan areas, while still offering the allure of suburban living. These suburban locales provide residents with a desirable quality of life characterized by tranquility, safety, and access to essential amenities. A well-chosen location attracts a steady stream of potential tenants seeking convenient access to employment centers, schools, shopping centers, recreational facilities, and other amenities. Proximity to major metros and transportation hubs enhances the appeal of the community, driving tenant demand and occupancy rates. Investing in build-to-rent properties in high-growth areas with strong economic fundamentals and favorable demographic trends can lead to significant property value appreciation over time. Locations with robust job markets, population growth, and infrastructure development tend to experience sustained appreciation in property values, enriching the long-term investment outlook. By identifying well-located sites that cater to the preferences and lifestyle needs of renters, developers can unlock the full potential of their BTR projects and create thriving communities that resonate with tenants.

In essence, prioritizing the quality of surrounding schools and educational centers is essential for the success of build-to-rent communities. By selecting sites in close proximity to top-ranked schools, we create environments where residents can thrive academically, socially, and economically, fostering a sense of pride, belonging, and long-term residency within the community. Good school districts play a vital role in fostering a sense of community and belonging among residents. By residing in neighborhoods with reputable schools, tenants develop strong ties to their surroundings and forge long-term relationships with neighbors who share similar values and aspirations. This sense of community pride and engagement contributes to the overall stability and vibrancy of the BTR community, creating an environment where residents feel invested in their homes and actively contribute to its success. In addition to primary and secondary schools, we also consider the proximity of BTR communities to junior colleges and higher education institutions. Access to quality higher education facilities further enhances the attractiveness of the neighborhood, catering to the needs of students, young professionals, and families seeking educational advancement opportunities. By offering convenient access to educational resources at every level, our BTR communities become sought-after destinations for individuals and families looking to invest in their future.

Sites that back up to commercial developments may detract from the residential feel of the community and can introduce noise, traffic, and visual disruptions. To maintain the ambiance of a traditional subdivision and enhance the quality of life for residents, we avoid locations that directly abut commercial properties. Development sites situated near RV parks, mobile home sites, manufacturing plants, or railroad tracks may experience increased noise levels, traffic congestion, and visual obstructions. These factors can diminish the appeal of the BTR community and deter potential renters seeking a tranquil residential environment. High crime rates in the vicinity of a potential BTR site can adversely affect the perceived safety and security of the neighborhood, leading to concerns among prospective renters and impacting rental demand. We conduct thorough assessments of crime statistics and neighborhood safety measures to mitigate risks and provide residents with peace of mind.

Let's review my top factors in determining the best possible land options for BTR communities:

Accessibility: Renters prefer properties that are easily accessible, especially to essential services such as transportation, grocery stores, healthcare facilities, and entertainment centers. Potential renters value convenience and accessibility.

Rental demand: By selecting a location with a high demand for rental properties, developers can ensure that their property will be occupied quickly and generate a steady rental income.

Competition: Developers should select a location with a lower supply of rental properties, which can reduce competition and increase the occupancy rates/absorption.

Demographics: Different neighborhoods have different demographics, and BTR developers need to take this into consideration. If a developer's target market is young business professionals, then a location close to urban centers and entertainment areas would be more attractive.

Property/land value: The location of a BTR property can affect its long-term valuation. Properties in desirable locations tend to appreciate in value over time and will provide better returns on investment.

Area Demographics

Indeed, understanding area demographics is essential for creating successful BTR communities that cater to the needs and preferences of the target population. Here are some key demographic factors to consider.

Age and family status of a population in the surrounding area can impact the demand for rental properties. For example, if the local population is mostly young business professionals, the community should be designed with amenities and features that appeal to that demographic, such as high-speed internet, fitness centers, and communal workspaces. Areas with a high proportion of young professionals or families may have a higher demand for rental properties.

Income levels influence the affordability of rental properties and the amenities that residents can afford. By understanding the income distribution in the area, developers can tailor BTR communities to meet the needs of various income brackets, offering a range of housing options and pricing structures.

The education level of residents can impact their housing preferences, lifestyle choices, and demand for certain amenities. Areas with a higher percentage of residents with college degrees or advanced degrees may prioritize access to cultural institutions, recreational facilities, and educational opportunities for their families.

Growth trends are also a very important factor to understand when evaluating future build-to-rent communities. Areas experiencing population growth may have a higher demand for rental properties, while areas experiencing population decline may be less attractive for long-term success. Demographic data on family size and household composition help developers design BTR communities that accommodate the diverse needs of residents. Communities with larger households may require more spacious floor plans and family-friendly amenities, while those with a higher concentration of single professionals may prioritize amenities such as coworking spaces and fitness centers.

Understanding the ethnic and cultural diversity of the local population enables developers to create inclusive and culturally sensitive environments that celebrate diversity and promote social cohesion. Offering amenities and programming that cater to diverse cultural backgrounds can enhance the sense of community and belonging within the BTR community. By analyzing area demographics comprehensively, developers can make informed decisions about site selection, design, and amenities, ensuring that BTR communities align with the preferences and needs of the target demographic and foster a vibrant and thriving residential environment.

Land Plot Size and Shape

When identifying raw land, plot size and shape requires a thorough site analysis and determination of setbacks and zoning requirements, infrastructure requirements, and market demand. Most of our current BTR communities are minimum twelve acres due to density restrictions and detention requirements. These steps can help identify the optimal plot size and shape that meets both the needs of the community and local regulations.

The first step is to conduct a site analysis. Before identifying the plot size and shape, a site analysis is conducted to determine the site's existing conditions, including its topography, soil conditions, vegetation, and access to utilities. This information can help determine the optimal size and shape of the development and help identify any constraints or opportunities that could impact the plot size and shape. Local zoning regulations often dictate the minimum lot size and shape requirements for residential developments, including BTR communities. Developers must ensure that the chosen plot complies with these regulations to obtain necessary permits and approvals. Additionally, setbacks, easements, and other zoning requirements may impact the usable space within the plot.

The next step is to determine the desired density of the build-to-rent community. The goal of any developer is to create a site plan with the smallest lots allowed depending on county and city regulations. The desired density should be informed by market demand, zoning regulations, and financial feasibility. The size and shape of the land plot influence the feasibility and cost of installing essential infrastructure such as roads, utilities, drainage systems, and landscaping. Larger plots may accommodate more efficient layout designs and infrastructure placement, while irregularly shaped plots may require creative solutions to optimize space and functionality.

Developers must also identify setbacks and infrastructure requirements. This information helps determine the maximum size and shape of the development. Infrastructure includes the roads, parking lots, utilities, amenities, and any detention requirements. The most important infrastructure requirement is access to all utilities (water/sewer). Local zoning ordinances specify setback requirements, which dictate the distance between structures and property lines. Developers must adhere to these regulations to ensure compliance and obtain necessary permits for construction. By identifying setbacks early in the planning process, developers can design the layout of the BTR community to maximize usable space within the designated boundaries. In addition to setbacks, local zoning requirements may include other development standards such as maximum building height, lot coverage, and building materials. Understanding these standards helps developers create designs that meet regulatory requirements while achieving the desired aesthetic and functionality for the BTR community.

Density Regulations and Parameters

Density regulations and parameters are important considerations for BTR communities, because they impact the maximum number of units that can be built on a site and affect the overall profitability of the development. The target number of units in all BTR communities varies from state to state, but in Texas all of our institutional partners are targeting projects around 100 to 150 property developments. The size of these developments is determined by population growth and current rental inventory. Here are some key factors to consider when evaluating density regulations and parameters for build-to-rent communities.

Density regulations are typically governed by local zoning ordinances, which prescribe the maximum number of units allowed per acre or lot size. These regulations are designed to ensure that developments are compatible with surrounding land uses, infrastructure capacity, and community character. Developers must review the zoning regulations applicable to the site to determine the permissible density and comply with the established parameters. Some jurisdictions offer density bonus programs that allow developers to exceed standard density limits in exchange for providing certain community benefits, such as affordable housing units, public open space, or infrastructure improvements. Developers may explore opportunities to leverage density bonuses to increase the number of units in their BTR communities while contributing to the overall livability and sustainability of the development.

Zoning regulations typically specify the maximum density for a given area. These regulations may be based on factors such as lot size, building height, setbacks, and parking requirements. The maximum density is often expressed as Floor Area Ratio (FAR), which sets the ratio of total floor area to the size of the lot. The FAR can impact the number of units that can be built on a given lot.

Building codes set a minimum standard for building safety, including minimum room sizes, ceiling heights, and egress requirements. Many municipalities have comprehensive plans that provide guidance on land use and development. These plans include recommendations on density levels for various types of development. Building codes can impact the overall layout and design of the units and common spaces in build-to-rent communities.

The density of a BTR community can contribute to increased traffic volumes on surrounding roadways, especially during peak commuting hours. Developers should assess the traffic impact of the proposed development and consider measures to mitigate congestion, such as implementing traffic-calming measures, improving road infrastructure, or providing alternative transportation options like bike lanes or public transit connections. Engaging with local transportation authorities and conducting traffic impact studies can help developers address potential traffic concerns and ensure the compatibility of the BTR development with existing transportation networks.

Finally, it's important to consider the financial feasibility of the proposed development. The level of density may impact the construction and development costs, as well as the potential profitability of the project. Higher density may be more profitable but may also require more complex financing structures and higher construction costs. It is important to conduct a thorough financial analysis to determine the optimal level of density for the development. Developers should carefully assess the cost implications of different density levels and consider factors such as land acquisition costs, materials, labor, permits, and fees when estimating construction and development expenses.

Access to Utilities

Access to utilities is a critical consideration for build-to-rent communities because it can impact the development and operation of the community. It can also impact the feasibility, cost, and overall quality of the development and satisfaction of tenants. Here are some reasons why access to utilities is so important.

Access to clean water, electricity, gas, and sewer systems is fundamental for providing basic necessities to tenants in BTR communities. These utilities are essential for cooking, bathing, heating, cooling, and sanitation purposes, ensuring that residents can live comfortably and safely in their homes. Developers must ensure that all necessary utilities are available and properly functioning before leasing units to tenants. Access to utilities also impacts the operational efficiency of BTR communities. Efficient water and energy systems can help minimize utility costs for property owners and tenants, making the development more economically sustainable in the long run. Energy-efficient appliances, lighting, and HVAC systems can reduce energy consumption and lower utility bills for residents, enhancing affordability and attractiveness of the community.

Efficient maintenance and repair processes help minimize downtime for BTR communities, ensuring that tenants can continue to enjoy uninterrupted access to essential utilities. Quick response times to maintenance requests and efficient resolution of issues contribute to the overall functionality and livability of the community. Minimizing downtime due to utility-related problems helps maintain tenant retention and prevents disruptions to daily routines and activities.

The cost of connecting to utilities can vary widely depending on the location and existing infrastructure. It's important to carefully assess the cost of connecting to utilities as part of the development budget.

In summary, developers should assess the availability, cost, and regulatory compliance requirements for utilities such as water, sewer, electricity, gas, and telecommunications. By ensuring access to these utilities, developers can create a safe, healthy, and desirable living environment for tenants, which is essential for long-term success of the development.

MUDs and PIDs

Municipal Utility Districts (MUDs) are special-purpose districts that can be created by the Texas legislature to finance and provide infrastructure, services, and facilities within designated areas. MUDs can issue bonds to fund the construction of water, sewer, drainage, and road infrastructure, as well as parks and recreational facilities. MUDs can also levy taxes and fees on property owners within the district to repay the bonds and fund ongoing operations.

Public Improvement Districts (PIDs) are special districts that can be created by local governments to finance and provide public improvements and services such as landscaping, street lighting, security, and marketing. PIDs can be funded by assessments on property owners within the district and can be administered by a board of directors appointed by local government.

Both MUDs and PIDs can be used in build-to-rent communities to finance the construction of public infrastructure improvements that benefit the community. These improvements can make the community more attractive to tenants and increase the long-term value of the development. However, it is important to note that the MUD and PID taxes are in addition to regular property taxes and can significantly impact the overall cost of owning or renting property within these districts. It is also important to carefully evaluate the financing terms and repayment schedules of any bonds issued by MUD or PID to ensure that the financing is financially feasible and sustainable over the long term.

In summary, MUDs and PIDs are special districts that can be used in build-to-rent communities to finance public infrastructure improvements. While they can provide significant benefits, it's important to carefully evaluate the potential costs and financing terms before using these districts in a development.

Easements, Setbacks

Easements are legal rights granted to individuals or entities to use a portion of a property for a specific purpose. Common examples include utility easements, which grant access to water, gas, or electrical lines. Pedestrian or bicycle easements allow access to public spaces or amenities. Easements can restrict the use of certain areas of a property and can impact the design and construction of a build-to-rent community. Indeed, easements play a significant role in the development of BTR communities, particularly in relation to setbacks and property usage. Here's how easements, setbacks, and property rights intersect in the context of BTR developments.

Utility easements are among the most common types of easements encountered in BTR projects. These easements grant utility companies the legal right to access, install, repair, and maintain utility infrastructure (such as water, gas, electricity, and telecommunications lines) that traverse the property. Developers must take these easements into account when planning the layout and construction of BTR communities to ensure that utility access is not obstructed and that any proposed structures comply with easement requirements.

Setbacks are intended to create open space between buildings and property lines or adjacent structures. This open space serves various purposes, including enhancing safety, promoting aesthetics, and preserving the character of the neighborhood. In BTR communities, setbacks help maintain a sense of openness and separation between individual units, contributing to a more appealing and livable environment for residents. Setbacks can influence the density, layout, and design of BTR developments by limiting the buildable area on the site. Larger setbacks may reduce the number of units that can be accommodated within the community or require adjustments to building configurations to maintain adequate separation. Additionally, setbacks may affect the orientation and arrangement of buildings within the site, influencing factors such as sunlight exposure, privacy, and views for residents.

Both easements and setbacks are important legal considerations when developing build-to-rent communities. Failure to comply with easements and setbacks can lead to legal disputes, fines, or other penalties, which will impact the profitability and viability of the community. By carefully reviewing and understanding the easements and setbacks on the property, and complying with the local zoning regulations, developers can create a community that meets legal requirements and maximizes profitability.

Zoning Requirements

Zoning regulations categorize land into different use classifications, such as residential, commercial, industrial, or mixed-use. BTR communities typically fall under residential zoning categories, which permit the construction of single-family homes, townhouses, or multifamily developments intended for rental occupancy. Developers must ensure that the proposed BTR project complies with the applicable zoning classification to obtain necessary permits and approvals. Here are some factors to consider when assessing zoning requirements for a build-to-rent community.

When developers are permitting a land site, zoning requirements dictate the permitted uses for a particular area, which can impact the type of BTR community that can be developed. For example, certain areas may be zoned for residential or commercial use only, which may limit the type of BTR community that can be developed.

Zoning ordinances typically prescribe setback requirements, which specify the minimum distance that buildings must be set back from property lines or adjacent structures. Additionally, lot coverage regulations may limit the percentage of the lot that can be occupied by buildings or impervious surfaces. Compliance with setback and lot coverage standards influences the design, orientation, and spatial arrangement of BTR structures within the development site.

By carefully evaluating and adhering to zoning requirements, developers can navigate regulatory constraints, obtain necessary approvals, and create successful BTR communities that meet regulatory standards, fulfill market demand, and provide desirable living environments for residents.

Rental Rates

Rental rate requirements for BTR communities can vary depending on several factors, including the location, market demand, and the quality of the community. Rental rate requirements are an important consideration when developing because they can impact the profitability and viability of the project. Here are some factors to consider when assessing rental requirements.

The rental rates for a BTR community are largely determined by the market demand for rental properties in the surrounding area. Understanding the target demographic and their preferences for unit size, amenities, and community features can help identify the optimal rental rates for the community. Position the BTR community strategically within the rental market segment to capture demand from specific tenant segments and optimize occupancy rates. Determine whether the community targets premium, midmarket, or affordable rental segments and adjust rental rates accordingly to align with market positioning and competitiveness.

The quality of the BTR community also impacts the rental rates. Rental rates should be set at a level that ensures tenant satisfaction. Determine the value proposition of the BTR community by identifying unique features, amenities, and services that differentiate it from competing rental properties. Highlight value-added amenities such as community facilities, recreational areas, maintenance services, and smart home technology to justify premium rental rates and enhance tenant satisfaction.

The target demographic for the BTR community can also impact rental rates. Consider the demographic profile and preferences of potential tenants when setting rental rates. Tailor rental pricing strategies to attract target demographics such as young professionals, families, empty nesters, or retirees based on their housing needs, lifestyle preferences, and willingness to pay for amenities and conveniences.

Finally, the financing feasibility to the BTR community can impact the rental rates. Higher rental rates may be required to support the financing structure of the community, which may include debt financing, equity financing, and return on investment for equity investors.

In summary, rental rate requirements for BTR communities are determined by a combination of market demand, community quality, target demographic, operating expenses, and financial feasibility. By carefully evaluating rental rate requirements and considering various factors influencing market demand, affordability, value proposition, and operational considerations, developers can establish competitive and sustainable rental rates for BTR communities that appeal to target tenants and support long-term financial viability.

Annual Rent Growth

Annual rent growth is a key performance metric for BTR communities. Rent growth refers to the increase of rental rates over time, typically expressed as a percentage. Rental growth is an important consideration to impact the profitability and long-term viability of the development. Key factors to consider when assessing annual rental growth for BTR communities include market demand and location.

Market demand for rental properties in the surrounding area will largely determine the rental growth of a community. Evaluate market demand dynamics, including population growth, employment trends, and housing supply constraints, to anticipate rental demand fluctuations and potential drivers of rent growth. Strong demand for rental properties in desirable locations with limited supply can lead to competitive rental markets and upward pressure on rental rates. Review historical rent growth trends and performance metrics for similar BTR communities in the market or comparable areas to identify patterns and forecast future rent growth potential. Analyzing past performance can provide insights into market dynamics and factors driving rent growth.

Location of the BTR community will always impact rental growth. Areas with strong economic growth, employment opportunities, and desirable amenities may be able to command higher rental growth rates. Consider the geographical location of the BTR community and its proximity to major employment centers, transportation hubs, educational institutions, and lifestyle amenities. Locations with high demand for rental housing and limited available land for development are more likely to experience higher rent growth rates over time.

In summary, annual rental growth for build-to-rent communities is determined by a combination of market demand, community quality, location, and rental rates. Developers should carefully assess each of these factors to determine the potential for rental growth over time and to maximize profitability.

Property Taxes

Property taxes can significantly impact the financial feasibility and profitability of BTR communities. Property taxes represent a significant operating expense for BTR communities, often ranking among the largest expenses alongside maintenance, utilities, and insurance. Higher property tax assessments and tax rates can increase operating costs, reducing net operating income and profitability for property owners. Here are some ways property taxes can affect build-to-rent communities.

> **Tax assessment:** Property taxes directly impact the financial performance and investment returns of BTR communities. Higher property taxes can lower the overall return on investment and diminish the attractiveness of the property as an investment opportunity. Developers and

investors should carefully analyze the potential impact of property taxes on cash flow and ROI projections.

Tax rate: Property tax rates can vary depending on the location and local government regulations. High property taxes can make a BTR community less marketable to potential tenants. Most of our development partners tend to stay away from any areas with a tax rate over 3 percent. Developers may explore various tax mitigation strategies to minimize property tax liabilities and optimize financial performance. This may include leveraging tax incentives, exemptions, or abatements or appealing tax assessments to reduce tax burdens and enhance property profitability.

Value of the property: Property taxes can also impact the value of the property. Higher property taxes can reduce the value of the property, making it more difficult to refinance or sell the property in the future. Property taxes are often based on the assessed value of the property, which can fluctuate over time due to changes in market conditions, property improvements, and reassessment cycles. Developers should consider the potential impact of property valuation changes on tax assessments and budget accordingly for future tax liabilities.

By carefully evaluating property tax considerations and incorporating them into financial analysis and planning processes, developers and investors can make informed decisions and optimize the financial performance and long-term sustainability of BTR communities.

Cost of Land

The cost of land directly influences the financial feasibility of developing a BTR community. Higher land costs require developers to generate greater rental revenue to cover expenses and achieve target returns on investment. Evaluating land costs relative to projected rental income is essential for determining the viability of a BTR project.

The cost of acquiring the land is a major expense for all developers. Most of our current developers must purchase the land for under four dollars per square foot since impact fees and entitlements costs have almost doubled over the last two years. Land costs affect the ROI of BTR developments by impacting the initial investment required and the potential return generated over time. Developers must analyze the relationship between land costs, rental income, operating expenses, and investment returns to assess the financial viability of the project and make informed investment decisions.

The cost of the land can also impact the construction costs of the BTR community. Higher land costs require developers to build more units on the land to achieve a sufficient return on investment, which will increase the construction costs. Developers may employ negotiation strategies to secure favorable land deals and mitigate the impact of high land costs on project profitability. This may include conducting thorough due diligence, exploring alternative financing options, leveraging incentives or concessions, and negotiating favorable terms with land sellers or property owners.

REMEMBER:

- ➡ Land selection is the first step in building a BTR community.

- ➡ Communities are outside major metropolitan areas and in the suburbs but within driving distance.

- ➡ Location is key and looks at schools, demographics, plot size, density, regulations, access to utilities, zoning, easements and setbacks, and neighborhood amenities.

- ➡ Land costs should be four dollars or less per square foot.

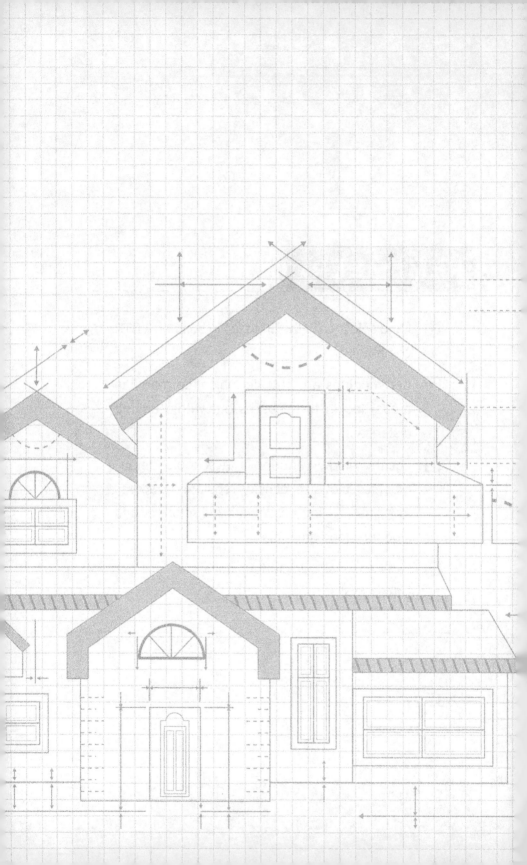

CHAPTER 4

THE TYPICAL FEASIBILITY PERIOD FOR A BUILD-TO-RENT CONTRACT

W inHill Advisors-Kirby plays a pivotal role, especially during the foundational stages of each project. This chapter delves into the typical feasibility period for a BTR contract, a phase where strategic decisions are made, setting the trajectory for a project's success. This stage is critical, not only for ensuring the financial and market feasibility of a project but also for aligning the interests of all stakeholders involved.

Bringing all parties to the table is the next critical step. This phase is about more than just negotiation; it's about creating a shared vision for what the project can achieve. Our role involves facilitating discussions between landowners, developers, investors, and any other stakeholders to ensure that everyone's interests and expectations are aligned. This alignment is crucial for moving forward with a purchase contract and ultimately dictates the project's progression from concept to reality.

The Letter of Intent (LOI) plays a critical role in the early stages of a BTR transaction, acting as the bridge between initial interest and formal agreement. In the complex and often nuanced field of real estate development, especially within the BTR sector, the LOI is a tool of paramount importance. It sets the foundation for negotiations, offering a structured outline of the key terms and conditions expected to form the core of the Purchase and Sales Agreement (PSA). At its core, the LOI signifies a mutual interest between the buyer and the seller to engage in a transaction under specified terms. It outlines the fundamental components of the deal, such as:

Purchase price: The LOI starts by stating the agreed-upon price or the formula that will be used to determine the final purchase price. This clarity is essential for both parties to assess the financial viability of the transaction.

Downpayment amounts: It specifies the initial deposit and any subsequent payments to be made before closing. This shows the buyer's commitment and helps the seller gauge the buyer's financial readiness.

Contingencies: These are conditions that must be met for the transaction to proceed. Common contingencies include financing, approval of the buyer's due diligence, and any specific legal or regulatory approvals that may be required for the development.

Feasibility period: The LOI outlines the timeframe allocated for due diligence, allowing the buyer to assess the site's suitability, market potential, and any development constraints. This period is crucial for the buyer to confirm that the project aligns with their investment criteria and objectives.

Closing conditions: The terms under which the deal will be finalized are stated, including any actions or approvals required from either party before the transaction can close.

Once the LOI is agreed upon and signed, it acts as the reference point for drafting the formal PSA. It's important to note that while the LOI itself is typically nonbinding (with the exception of certain provisions like confidentiality), it represents a significant step toward finalizing the transaction. The goodwill and understanding established during this phase are invaluable, laying the groundwork for a successful partnership and project.

The transition from a signed LOI to the drafting of the PSA marks a significant progression in the BTR transaction process. The process begins with the buyer's attorneys translating the terms outlined in the LOI into a comprehensive PSA. This document serves as the definitive agreement between the buyer and the seller, encompassing all aspects of the transaction. The PSA is more than a legal formality; it is a comprehensive blueprint that guides the BTR transaction from agreement to action. The feasibility period, in particular, is a testament to the complexity and collaborative nature of BTR projects, requiring a meticulous approach to due diligence and planning. By understanding and effectively navigating this phase, developers and investors can mitigate risks and lay a solid foundation for successful BTR developments.

What's Involved in a Feasibility Period

The feasibility period is a critical stage in the BTR contract process, and several key considerations come into play. The primary objective of the feasibility period is to evaluate the financial and operational feasibility of the proposed build-to-rent development. Developers and investors undertake comprehensive analyses to determine whether the project makes good business and financial sense. During this period various factors are examined to assess the potential risks, challenges, and profitability of the project. These considerations help investors to make informed decisions and evaluate the project's viability from different angles.

One of the most important factors in any BTR community is a market analysis. This analysis includes in-depth study on rental demand, market trends, competitive landscape, and rental benchmarks. A comprehensive financial analysis is also conducted to evaluate the potential return on investment. This involves estimating construction costs, operating expenses, and rental income and forecasting cash flows to determine the project's profitability and viability for investors. A thorough market analysis is fundamental to assess the demand for a BTR development in the proposed location. Technology has started to play a pivotal role in providing updated data for demographic studies to understand the characteristics of local population and lifestyle preferences. It can also analyze local and regional economic indicators such as employment growth, income levels, and migration patterns.

The design and construction examination during the feasibility process is a comprehensive evaluation that spans the initial visual and functional aspects of the project to the final touches that define the tenant experience. Developers and investors review architectural plans, engineering requirements, and construction estimates to determine if any changes need to be made to the design layout of the community. Developers also consider the feasibility of delivering a seamless tenant experience, including amenities, services, and technological infrastructure.

The feasibility period is a rigorous evaluation phase that lays the groundwork for a successful BTR project. By thoroughly assessing market conditions, financial viability, site characteristics, legal and regulatory compliance, and potential risks, developers and investors can proceed with confidence, knowing that their project is built on a solid foundation of comprehensive analysis and strategic planning.

Before the buyer can conduct their due diligence, they need to receive from the seller the following documents within a certain number of days after the contract is executed. These documents, tests, and other materials can reduce the seller's liability and the buyer's risk, and even increase the land value:

Title reports: These reveal the legal rights of ownership to the property; issues with a title such as liens, competing claims, or other concerns will surface with title reports.

Maintenance records: These can reveal whether work has been done on the land, which may make it more viable for building.

Leases: These can show whether the land is committed for a time period that may deter development to the buyer's expectations.

Property studies and surveys: These can reveal any easements, encroachments, or other similar issues.

Environmental and soil reports that the seller already possesses: These can reveal whether the land is in a flood zone or has drainage issues, whether the soil can be built on, the presence of endangered species or ground contamination, and other issues that can prevent the project from moving forward.

Violation notices: Violations will need to be resolved before development begins.

Feasibility periods can last anywhere from sixty days at minimum all the way up to a year, depending on what reports and what type of engineering studies have been done prior to us making an offer on the property. Feasibility periods that are done in around sixty days typically apply to projects with no restrictions and no density regulations. In these cases, the feasibility period is focused on validating existing reports, confirming the project's financial and market viability, and finalizing preliminary design and construction estimates. A true raw land deal, where little to no prior due diligence has been performed, necessitates a full range of studies, including environmental assessments, soil testing, and market demand analysis. For raw land, detailed engineering studies and architectural plans need to be developed from scratch. This includes assessing the site's suitability for construction, infrastructure planning, and ensuring compliance with all regulatory requirements.

Here is some sample language regarding feasibility periods from a BTR contract.

Section 4.01 Due Diligence Materials. Seller shall make available to Buyer copies of the following documents and materials pertaining to the Property within (7) days from the Effective Date, to the extent within Seller's possession or control: title commitment/policy, survey, site plans and specifications, architectural plans, inspections, environmental/hazardous material reports, soils reports, governmental permits/approvals, zoning information, tax information and utility letters, certificate(s) of occupancy, warranties and guaranties, commission agreements, and other similar materials relating to the physical and environmental condition of the Property, and any other documents relating to the Property reasonably requested by Buyer (collectively, the "**Due Diligence Materials**").

Section 4.02 Due Diligence Period. Buyer shall have a period, commencing on the Effective Date through the date which is sixty (60) days after the Effective Date (the "**Due Diligence Period**"), to conduct or cause to be conducted any and all tests, studies, surveys, inspections, reviews, assessments, or evaluations of the Property, including without limitation engineering, topographic, soils, zoning, wetlands, and environmental inspections (including Phase I and/or Phase II environmental site assessments to be performed by an environmental consultant selected by Buyer) (the "**Inspections**"), as Buyer deems necessary, desirable, or appropriate in its sole and absolute discretion, and analysis of the Due Diligence Materials....

Section 4.04 Delivery of Diligence Materials.... At any time prior to the Final Closing (including during the Due Diligence Period), and at all times, subject to the terms of this Agreement. Buyer and its agents, employees, consultants, inspectors, appraisers, engineers, and contractors (collectively, "**Buyer's Representatives**") shall have the right to visit the Property during normal business hours by appointment with the Seller, to examine and inspect the same, as well as conduct reasonable tests, studies, investigations, and surveys to assess utility availability, soil conditions, environmental conditions, physical condition, and the like of the Property.

Section 4.06 Buyer's Right to Inspect. In connection with such Inspections, neither Buyer nor any of Buyer's Representatives shall unreasonably interfere with the business of Seller conducted at the Property. Buyer shall schedule and coordinate all Inspections or other access thereto with Seller. Seller shall be entitled to have a representative present at all times during each such inspection or other access. Seller shall allow Buyer and Buyer's Representatives unlimited access to the Property and to other information pertaining thereto in the possession or within the control of Seller.

The feasibility period is a foundational phase in the development of BTR projects, setting the stage for a successful and viable development. Its duration is heavily influenced by the specifics of the property in question and the extent of preparatory work previously conducted. Whether a project benefits from a shorter feasibility period due to minimal restrictions and comprehensive preliminary studies or requires a longer timeline to navigate the complexities of raw land development, a methodical and informed approach during this phase is crucial to laying the groundwork for a successful project outcome.

Real Estate Entitlements During Feasibility

Real estate entitlements are at the heart of the development process, acting as a pivotal factor in the feasibility period of a real estate project, especially within the BTR sector. These entitlements, essentially permissions granted by governmental or regulatory bodies, dictate whether and how a parcel of land can be developed. They encompass a wide range of approvals, including zoning variances, land-use designations, building permits, and utility approvals, among others. Understanding and securing these entitlements is a critical step that can significantly influence the timeline, cost, and overall feasibility of a development project. Here's a closer look at their significance and the considerations they entail during the feasibility period.

Entitlements are a primary determinant of a project's viability. They confirm that a developer can legally proceed with their intended use of the land, be it constructing a new BTR community, redeveloping an existing property, or altering the land use. Entitlements also determine the density allowed based on county and city regulations. BTR developers look for development sites that have few or no restrictions regarding lot minimum size requirements to maximize the amount of homes in each community.

Developers must identify specific entitlements necessary for each proposed project, and these can vary widely depending on the nature and scope of the project. Common types of entitlements include zoning changes, conditional use permits, variances, environmental impact reports, subdivision approvals, building permits, and utility approvals. The feasibility period allows developers or investors to understand the specific entitlements needed and evaluate the likelihood of obtaining them based on the project's scope and local regulations. Securing building permits is a straightforward concept but can be a complex process depending on the jurisdiction. Similarly, ensuring access to essential utilities like water, sewage, electricity, and internet—and obtaining any necessary permits for connecting these services—is a critical step that must be addressed during the feasibility period.

Many entitlement processes involve public hearings and opportunities for community input. Garnering community support can be pivotal for a project's approval, especially in areas where development is contentious or highly regulated. Engaging with the community early and often can facilitate smoother approval processes.

The feasibility period also allows developers/investors to estimate the timeline of completion and the cost associated with obtaining real estate entitlements. The process of obtaining entitlements can be lengthy and expensive, involving numerous fees, studies, and potentially legal challenges. During the feasibility period, developers should account for these factors in their project timelines and budgets, ensuring that they have allocated sufficient resources to navigate this phase.

Requirements for entitlements generally originate with the general plan of the city or county where the land is located and include current and future use and development requirements for the property. These help determine the activities that can take place on the land today and in the future and establish requirements for additional regulations on the land, such as zoning, building codes, compliance, and more.

For instance, a piece of land may be zoned residential but then also have regulations regarding types of construction materials used, heights of buildings, and more. Some areas have building codes that require compliance with an architectural review board or may have restrictions and conditions for properties built on the site. Permits may also be required for any grading or landscaping at the site, or for any building or remodeling; these permits ensure that all revisions to a site comply with existing requirements and that inspections are performed to verify compliance while improvements are in process and completed.

The developer of the property is responsible for acquiring entitlements. Developers often require entitlements to be in place before purchasing a property. They often prefer an option contract or extended escrow that gives them access to the property and enough time to obtain entitlements before escrow closes.

One of the biggest entitlement issues we typically encounter is in regard to water: Does the site have water and wastewater capacity for the development? The availability of water and wastewater capacity will determine the size of the development. Often, during the feasibility period, we'll find that there is not the capacity for the number of homes we envisioned for the BTR. It's crucial to understand what the city engineering department will allow regarding details such as how far the various lines have to be pulled (for water and wastewater). Then they go through a budget and planning session to map out how much it's going to cost and what the city is responsible for in the development of that site. If water or wastewater capacity is pending, then the developer may not be as interested in the site knowing the timeframe it's going to take to get that completely approved through all your entitlements.

Another issue is ensuring that the plan drawn up by the architect, which should include all plots, amenities, streets, etc., can be approved by city engineering and planning departments. The site plan must be shown to the city engineering department, and it must receive approval.

If there is not a MUD or a PID, developers may have to create one. Developing a MUD is not an easy process; it can take a year or even two.

Infrastructure costs are part of a feasibility study. These can sometimes seem infinite and range from installing roads, street signs, and fire hydrants to putting in fiber optics—basically anything that is placed in the ground. Infrastructure costs can also encompass amenities that can be monetized, such as dog parks, walking trails, swimming pools, or clubhouses. Depending on the location, site conditions, labor and materials, permit fees, and hookup charges, site development costs can vary greatly.

The costs for infrastructure are based on how many homes are built. A development of fewer than one hundred homes does not need to be monetized—no swimming pool, clubhouse, or gym. Instead, as mentioned in a previous chapter, most BTRs that we are involved in have water detention and a walking trail around that detention—that's it. Over one hundred home sites, especially in Arizona and Florida, have a pool, clubhouse, gym, volleyball court, or some other monetized areas based on demographics, whether the younger adults or senior retirees. But most of the time we try to keep the amenities at the lowest possible costs because we don't want any deferred maintenance. Pools, clubhouses, and gyms all have to be cleaned and monitored, and there are liabilities that need to be insured.

Once all the plans are submitted to the city—the engineering report, report on wastewater, site plan, and construction plans—then the city reviews them and determines whether there are any restrictions that cannot be approved. For instance, there may be restrictions on building two-story homes in that area.

The builder has its own building team, and they typically communicate their plans to the city development and planning department, and obtain all approvals. The developers we work with have completed multiple types of projects, so they have an efficient and effective working rapport with the cities and counties where they work; they already have their relationships built and understand whom they need to talk to in order to get things approved quickly. Alternatively, they may hire a third-party person to handle everything with the city; there are companies that handle the reports to the city council members. But in most cases, it's the development team that handles most of the approval process within the city.

Termination Period

The termination period in a build-to-rent contract refers to the specific timeframe during which either party (buyer and seller) has the right to terminate the contract without incurring significant penalties or breaching contractual obligations. This provision allows for flexibility and protection for both parties in case certain conditions or contingencies are not met and provides a window of opportunity to either party to exit the contract. This period also allows both parties to evaluate the project's feasibility, conduct due diligence, secure financing, and make a final decision based on the outcomes.

The duration of the termination period is typically negotiated and agreed upon by the buyer and seller during the contract negotiation stage. The length of the termination period can vary depending on the complexity of the transaction, the size of the project, and several other factors.

The termination period provisions in a BTR contract typically outline the specific procedures and requirements for terminating the contract. This includes the method of communication (written notice), the party responsible for initiating the termination, and any documentation or supporting evidence required to justify the termination. It is essential for both parties to comply with the contract provisions to ensure a smooth and legally valid termination process.

This cancellation option typically requires earnest money to be paid by the buyer; if the seller is notified within the specified number of days, then the earnest money can be refunded, minus any negotiated amount that the buyer agreed to pay for the contract cancellation option. If the contract is not cancelled, then the earnest money goes toward the purchase price and is factored into the closing equation.

Here is some typical language regarding termination rights in a BTR contract:

Section 4.03 Termination by Buyer During Due Diligence Period. Buyer shall have the unconditional right, for any reason or no reason whatsoever, to terminate this Agreement upon written notice to Seller delivered at any time prior to 11:59 p.m. EST on the last day of the Due Diligence Period. If Buyer does not timely notify Seller of its election to terminate this Agreement prior to 11:59 p.m. EST on the last day of the Due Diligence Period, Buyer shall be deemed to have elected to proceed in accordance with this Agreement, subject to the terms and conditions of this Agreement. If Buyer elects to terminate this Agreement … Escrow Holder shall return the Deposit to Buyer, and upon such refund being made, this Agreement shall terminate, and the Parties shall have no further liability hereunder (except with respect to those obligations hereunder which expressly survive the termination of this Agreement). Notwithstanding anything to the contrary contained in this Agreement, amendments to this Agreement to extend the Due Diligence Period may be agreed upon in writing by each Party and notices to terminate this Agreement prior to the expiration of the Due Diligence Period may be given, by Buyer as provided in this Agreement by fax or by email to Seller....

Section 4.07 Termination Rights. If, as a result of Buyer's investigation of the Property and review of the Due Diligence Materials, Buyer, in its sole and absolute discretion, decides not to purchase the Property, Buyer shall indicate such approval by delivering written notice thereof to Seller and the Escrow Holder at any time prior to the expiration of the Due Diligence Period (the "**Termination Notice**"). At any time during the Due Diligence Period, Buyer may deliver the Termination Notice to Seller and Escrow Holder. Should Seller and Escrow Holder not receive the Termination Notice prior to the expiration of the Due Diligence Period, Buyer shall conclusively be deemed to have approved its investigation of the Property and to have elected to purchase the Property. In the event that this Agreement is terminated pursuant to this Section, Escrow Holder shall subtract from the First Deposit, the Independent Consideration and all fees, termination charges and title changes for the Escrow Holder and shall return the balance of the First Deposit to Buyer, and Buyer shall return to Seller all of the Due Diligence Materials, and any and all copies thereof.

The differences between traditional commercial contracts and purchase sales contracts tailored for BTR projects are significant, reflecting the unique nature and scale of BTR developments. Unlike traditional commercial or residential deals, which often focus on single properties or parcels of land, BTR contracts encompass a broader scope, including multiple homes and extensive development efforts. Understanding these distinctions is crucial for anyone involved in BTR transactions because it impacts negotiation, financing, and project management strategies. Purchase sales contracts for BTR projects are distinct from traditional commercial contracts, reflecting the complexity and scale of these developments. They require careful negotiation and detailed planning to address the comprehensive costs, financing structures, risk management, and long-term operational considerations unique to building and managing rental communities. For developers and BTR clients alike, understanding these differences is essential for successful project execution and long-term profitability.

Financing for BTRs is different as well. Next, let's look at how these investors typically finance BTRs.

REMEMBER:

➡ Before the buyer can conduct their due diligence, they need to receive from the seller a number of documents to help determine the land's viability for development.

➡ Feasibility periods can last from sixty days to a year.

➡ Obtaining real estate entitlements is a crucial step in ensuring allowable use of land.

➡ Contracts typically include a termination period.

CHAPTER 5

DEBT & EQUITY REQUIREMENTS FOR FUNDING

F inancing is the lifeblood of any real estate development project, and this holds especially true for BTR projects, which often entail substantial upfront investments for land acquisition, construction, and long-term operations. The complex financial landscape of BTR developments requires a balanced approach to debt and equity financing, ensuring the project is not only viable but also profitable over the long term. Financing needs to be considered during the feasibility period, when calculations for materials are being put together, and before the site plan is approved. In this chapter, we delve into the intricacies of securing funding for BTR projects, highlighting the importance of debt and equity requirements and the strategic selection of financial partners and development teams.

At the core of BTR project financing is the blend of debt and equity. This mix determines not only the project's initial feasibility but also its long-term financial health. Choosing the right financial partners—those who understand the BTR market and can offer terms that align with the project's timeline and cash flow projections—is crucial during this phase. Similarly, assembling a development team with a proven track record in BTR projects like WinHill Advisors can enhance a project's attractiveness to lenders and investors.

Debt Financing for Build-to-Rent Projects

Traditional bank loans are a common source of debt financing for build-to-rent projects. These loans are typically secured by the property itself, thorough evaluation of the financial feasibility of the project, market demand, rental income projections, and other factors we discussed in previous chapters. The most important factor in obtaining a traditional bank loan in today's economic climate is experience. It is almost impossible to get bank financing without a stellar track record of performance. Banks may offer competitive interest rates and terms, but they often have strict criteria and require a substantial down payment or equity contribution. The key advantage of debt financing is the ability to leverage a larger amount of capital while retaining control over the project. However, it also introduces fixed obligations in the form of interest payments and requires careful management to ensure that cash flows from the rental units can cover these costs.

Construction loans are a critical component of the financing strategy for BTR projects, offering the flexibility and staged funding necessary to support the dynamic and phased nature of construction projects. Funds are typically disbursed in stages or "draws" as construction milestones are reached, rather than as a lump sum. This staged funding approach aligns with the project's cash flow needs, ensuring that capital is available as required for each phase of development. Given the higher risk associated with construction projects, interest rates for these loans are generally higher than those for traditional mortgages. The rates can be fixed or variable, depending on the loan agreement. We have recently seen some of our institutional partners offering to take out the bank construction financing with the cost of capital currently. This allows the developer to deliver a product at a reduced price to the end user. By carefully navigating these financing options and building strategic partnerships, developers can enhance the viability and success of their BTR projects.

Mezzanine financing has emerged as a crucial tool in the capital stack of BTR projects, providing a flexible financing solution that sits between senior debt and equity in terms of priority and risk. This type of financing is particularly valuable in scenarios where developers seek to minimize their upfront equity investment while maximizing the project's overall funding. Let's delve into the characteristics of mezzanine financing, its benefits, and considerations for developers in the BTR sector.

Mezzanine financing is subordinate to senior debt, such as a mortgage or construction loan, but has priority over equity investments. This positioning reflects its higher risk compared to senior debt but lower risk relative to pure equity. Unlike senior debt, which is often secured by physical assets (e.g., land, buildings), mezzanine financing is usually secured by the ownership interests in the developer's entity, making it a form of quasi-equity. A distinctive feature of mezzanine loans is the option for lenders to convert their debt into equity in the project under certain conditions. This conversion feature provides a potential upside for lenders while offering developers a way to manage cash flow more effectively. Mezzanine financing is a powerful tool for BTR project financing, offering a blend of debt and equity characteristics that can enhance leverage, reduce capital requirements, and provide strategic advantages. By carefully integrating mezzanine financing into the capital stack, developers can navigate the complex funding landscape of BTR projects more effectively, driving projects forward while managing risk and optimizing returns. Working with specialized firms that understand the nuances of mezzanine financing in the BTR sector can be instrumental in achieving these goals.

Equity Financing for Build-to-Rent Projects

Equity financing forms a cornerstone of the funding structure for BTR projects, acting as a tangible demonstration of the developer's commitment and a critical lever for securing additional financing. The equity component not only aligns the interests of developers with the project's success but also reassures lenders and investors of the developer's confidence and stake in the project's outcomes. Here, we'll explore the nuances of equity financing in BTR projects, including sources of equity, expectations from lenders, and the strategic considerations for developers.

Developer equity can originate from various channels, reflecting the diverse approaches to capital accumulation and investment strategies within the real estate sector. While the exact percentage can vary depending on the project's specifics and the risk appetite of lenders, many experienced developers aim for a baseline equity contribution of around 35 percent of the total project cost. This figure strikes a balance between demonstrating substantial commitment and retaining enough liquidity to manage project contingencies and leverage additional financing opportunities.

Joint ventures and partnerships in the BTR sector are strategic alliances that leverage the strengths, resources, and expertise of multiple parties to undertake large-scale and often complex projects. These collaborative efforts can significantly enhance a project's viability, offering access to additional capital, diversified risk, and a combination of skills and networks that might be beyond the reach of individual participants acting alone. Let's delve into the dynamics of forming joint ventures or partnerships for BTR projects, highlighting the benefits, considerations, and key elements of successful collaborations.

One of the most immediate benefits of a joint venture is the ability to pool financial resources, providing the necessary equity and investment to move a project forward without overleveraging any single participant. BTR projects, with their significant upfront costs and long development timelines, entail considerable risk. By sharing this risk among partners, each entity can mitigate its exposure while still participating in a potentially lucrative venture. Collaborating with partners can bring together a diverse set of skills, industry knowledge, and networks, from local market insights to specialized legal and financial acumen, contributing to a more informed and strategic approach to development. Partnerships can lead to operational efficiencies through the sharing of responsibilities, from project management and construction to marketing and tenant management, leveraging each partner's core competencies.

The BTR sector has garnered substantial interest from institutional investors, including pension funds, Real Estate Investment Trusts (REITs), private equity firms, and insurance companies. This interest is driven by the sector's ability to offer stable, long-term income streams, making it an attractive investment compared to more volatile investment options. Institutional investors' involvement in BTR projects not only facilitates the development of large-scale communities but also aligns their investment strategies with the growing demand for rental housing. By participating in the funding and development process, institutional investors can influence the project's cost structure, achieving a lower cost basis for each unit and enhancing the project's profitability. The ability to lower the overall project costs can lead to higher rental yields and increased capital appreciation potential, thereby enhancing the return on investment for these institutional players. The increasing involvement of institutional investors in the BTR sector reflects the attractiveness of this asset class as a stable, long-term investment. For developers, partnering with such investors can provide the necessary capital to bring projects to fruition while benefiting from the expertise and networks that these investors bring. For institutional investors, BTR projects offer a compelling addition to their portfolios, promising steady returns in a sector that continues to demonstrate strong demand. As the BTR sector evolves, the synergy between institutional investors and developers is likely to play a pivotal role in shaping its future growth and development.

Successful funding of any BTR project requires a careful blend of debt and equity financing. Developers need to consider financing capabilities, project feasibility, and risk tolerance when determining the optimal funding mix. Working closely with lenders, investors, and real estate partners can help developers secure the necessary capital to bring their BTR projects to fruition. It is crucial to conduct thorough financial analysis, market research, and due diligence to attract the right funding partners.

How Institutional Investors Fund BTRs

Institutional investors play a pivotal role in funding BTR projects, leveraging their substantial financial resources to provide both equity capital and debt financing. This dual approach to investment allows institutional investors to engage deeply with the BTR sector, capitalizing on its growth and stability. Let's explore the mechanisms through which institutional investors fund BTR projects, highlighting the advantages and strategic considerations of both equity and debt financing.

Equity financing from institutional investors involves injecting capital into a BTR project in exchange for an ownership stake. This method of financing is crucial for covering significant upfront costs associated with BTR developments. Beyond equity investments, institutional investors may also provide debt financing to BTR projects. This can take the form of loans with terms that are often more competitive than what traditional banks offer. Institutional investors interested in the sector may seek long-term relationships, offering financing terms that reflect a mutual interest in the project's success.

Institutional investors are indispensable to the financing ecosystem of BTR projects, offering both equity capital and debt financing to support development. By providing the necessary upfront capital and competitive financing options, these investors not only enable the realization of large-scale BTR projects but also contribute to the sector's overall growth and stability. For developers, tapping into institutional capital requires a strategic approach, balancing the benefits of access to substantial funds with the need to maintain project control and align with the right partners.

The strategy involving institutional investors purchasing BTR projects at the certificate of occupancy (CO) stage, coupled with placing deposits of 10 to 15 percent of the overall development costs, presents a streamlined and risk-mitigated approach to real estate development, particularly in the Texas market. This approach delineates clear benefits for both developers and institutional investors, leveraging the strengths and minimizing the risks inherent to each party. Here's a closer look at how this strategy works and its implications for BTR projects.

Institutional investors step in at a pivotal moment in the development lifecycle, the CO stage, which signifies that the project has been completed according to the relevant codes and regulations and is ready for occupancy. By committing to purchasing at this stage, institutional investors avoid the complexities and uncertainties associated with the construction phase, focusing instead on the investment's long-term income-generating potential. Recognizing the value of stepping into a ready-to-occupy project and the assurance of quality and compliance provided by the CO, institutional investors are often willing to pay a premium. This premium compensates the developer for the risks undertaken during the development phase.

For developers, this arrangement provides several key benefits. The Purchase and Sales Agreement (PSA) with an institutional investor provides a guarantee of sale, enhancing the developer's ability to secure traditional bank financing for the project. Lenders are more inclined to offer favorable terms when there's a clear exit strategy and a guaranteed buyer at the end of the development process. Developers can plan their projects with a clear understanding of the timeline and financials, minimizing the risks associated with market fluctuations or prolonged holding periods. By selling off completed projects to institutional investors, developers can quickly recoup their investment and redeploy capital into new opportunities, fostering a cycle of continuous development and growth. The approach of institutional investors purchasing BTR projects at the CO stage, backed by deposits and guaranteed sales agreements, exemplifies a strategic collaboration model in real estate development. It underscores the mutual benefits of risk mitigation for investors and financial assurance for developers, facilitating the continued growth and viability of the BTR sector, especially in markets like Texas where such strategies are increasingly becoming the norm.

Institutional investors contribute substantial funding to the BTR sector through equity investments, debt financing, joint ventures, direct investments in BTR platforms, and participation in securitization structures. Their involvement helps fuel the growth of the BTR market by providing developers with the necessary capital to acquire land, construct properties, and establish rental operations. The partnership between institutional investors and BTR developers creates opportunities for both parties to achieve their investment objectives and capitalize on the long-term income potential of the BTR sector.

Sometimes Financing Needs to Be Creative

Creative financing becomes not just an option but a necessity in the BTR sector, especially when dealing with the inherent challenges of funding new developments without an established operating history. The reluctance of traditional banks and some institutional investors to engage with projects perceived as higher risk requires developers to think outside the box and leverage alternative financing avenues. Let's delve into some of these creative financing strategies and how they can be applied to BTR developments.

BTR developments often lack an established operating history, especially for new projects. This can make it challenging to get secure traditional bank loans or attract institutional investors who typically prefer a proven track record. In such cases, developers may need to explore alternative financing options, such as private lenders or joint ventures with experienced partners, who are willing to take on the perceived higher risk associated with a new BTR project. Private lenders often provide more flexible financing options than traditional banks. They are typically more willing to consider the potential of a BTR project rather than focusing solely on existing cash flows or operating history. This flexibility can come at a cost, with higher interest rates reflecting the increased risk. However, for developers confident in their project's success, private lending can offer a viable path forward.

BTR developments typically require significant upfront capital for land acquisition, construction, and development of amenities and community features. Traditional financing sources may not be sufficient to meet these capital requirements. Developers may need to consider creative financing structures, such as mezzanine financing, where a combination of equity and debt is sure to bridge the gap between the developer's capital and senior debt. This allows the development team to leverage their equity and reduce upfront cash investment. Additionally, mezzanine lenders may be willing to take a more nuanced view of the project's potential, focusing on future cash flows and the developer's track record on similar projects.

BTR developments can include various property types, such as multifamily buildings, townhomes, or single-family homes within a larger community. These unique property types may not fit traditional underwriting models used by lenders, making it difficult to secure conventional financing. The first step in securing financing for BTR developments that don't fit traditional models is to identify lenders or investors with specific experience in the BTR sector. These entities are more likely to understand the unique value proposition of BTR projects and be familiar with the market dynamics that affect their profitability and risk profiles.

Financing requirements for BTR developments can vary depending on the local market dynamics, including supply and demand factors, rental market conditions, and regulatory consider-ations. In markets with high competition or restrictive regulations, securing traditional financing may be more challenging. Developers need to explore alternative funding sources such as local government incentives, grants, reimbursements, and public-private partnerships to make their BTR projects financially viable. Certain government programs offer loans for residential developments that can be applied to BTR projects. These loans might come with more favorable interest rates or terms.

Creative financing becomes necessary for BTR developments when traditional financing sources are limited, higher capital require-ments exist, unique property types are involved, repurposing or adaptive reuse is required, local market dynamics are challenging, or green building initiatives are prioritized. Exploring alternative financing options, partnering with experienced investors, and tailoring financing structures to the specific needs of BTR projects can help developers overcome these challenges and unlock the necessary capital to bring their projects to fruition. Other options include combining different types of financing, such as senior debt, mezzanine financing, and equity investments, to cover different aspects of the project's cost.

Other Sources of Financing

Alternative sources of financing for BTR projects can provide addi-tional options for developers to secure the necessary capital. Here are alternative sources of financing:

- Real estate crowdfunding platforms have emerged as a novel way to raise funds for BTR projects. By pooling money from a large number of investors, crowdfunding allows for smaller, individual investments to collectively fund a significant portion of a project. This method can democratize real estate investing, allowing smaller investors to participate in larger projects and providing developers with an alternative source of capital.

- Real estate syndication involves pooling funds from multiple investors to finance a BTR project. Syndication can be structured in various ways, such as limited partnerships or limited liability companies (LLCs). This method allows developers to access capital from individuals or groups interested in real estate investment but who may not have the means to undertake a project individually.

- Government programs and incentives can offer financing options for BTR projects. These projects include low-interest loans, grants, tax credits, or subsidies aimed at promoting affordable housing or community development.

- Seller financing is another option where the developer can negotiate financing arrangements with the property owner. This involves the property owner acting as the lender, providing financing for the BTR project.

- Community Development Financial Institutions (CDFIs) are specialized financial institutions that focus on providing capital to underserved communities and projects with community impact. These institutions offer loans, grants, and other financial services specifically designed to support affordable housing, community development, and revitalization efforts.

Financing BTR developments with unique property types requires a nuanced approach that goes beyond traditional lending models. By identifying experienced lenders or investors, leveraging specialized financing programs, employing creative deal structuring, and effectively communicating the project's strengths, developers can secure the necessary capital to bring these innovative and diverse BTR projects to fruition. WinHill Advisors can help navigate these waters to align the best partnerships.

How Institutional Investors Fund BTRs

Institutional investors play a pivotal role in the financing, management, and ownership of BTR developments. These entities, which range from US-based to international private equity groups, deploy a variety of funding strategies to invest in BTR projects. Their ability to utilize vast reserves of capital—sourced from diverse avenues such as private equity, corporate partnerships, insurance leverage, and family offices—provides them with a significant edge in the real estate investment landscape. As interest rates fluctuate, these investors adapt their strategies to ensure their investments remain viable and meet their yield requirements. Let's explore the mechanisms through which institutional investors fund BTR developments and the impact of changing interest rates on their investment calculus.

Many institutional investors raise funds through private equity groups, pooling capital from high-net-worth individuals, pension funds, and other institutional investors to finance large-scale BTR projects. Collaborations with Fortune 500 companies can provide a steady influx of capital, often earmarked for real estate development projects that align with the corporations' strategic interests or housing needs for their employees. Some investors borrow against insurance policies, taking advantage of the lower interest rates available through these instruments to fund real estate investments. This method can provide substantial liquidity with relatively low cost.

Cross-collateralization is a sophisticated financial strategy employed by some investors, particularly in the real estate sector, to leverage existing assets for further investments or to secure better financing terms. By using the equity in properties that already generate substantial yields—over 10 percent, in the case of some single-family homes—investors can unlock additional capital to invest in new projects or enhance their investment portfolio. Institutions like Deutsche Bank or Blackstone often act as lending partners in such arrangements, providing the financial backing necessary for these complex transactions. Cross-collateralization can accelerate portfolio growth, allowing investors to leverage existing assets to finance new acquisitions or developments without needing to liquidate existing investments. Cross-collateralization is a powerful strategy for real estate investors looking to expand their portfolios or secure better financing terms by leveraging the equity in existing, high-yield properties. While it offers the potential for significant portfolio growth and improved loan conditions, it also requires careful consideration of the associated risks and complexities. Partnering with experienced financial institutions can help navigate these challenges, providing the expertise and support necessary to successfully leverage this strategy.

The strategy of leveraging existing real estate assets through appraisal and subsequent equity extraction is a key financial maneuver used by investors to fuel portfolio expansion and enhance returns. This approach, often facilitated by large lenders, capitalizes on the equity built up in properties, allowing investors to reinvest in new opportunities and further stabilize their investment portfolio. Here's how this process works and its implications for real estate investment strategies.

Investors start by getting an appraisal on their current properties, considering factors like purchase price, rental income, occupancy
status, and overall market conditions. This appraisal reflects the
current market value of the properties, often showing a significant
increase over the purchase price due to appreciation and improvements made to the properties. Based on the appraisal, big lenders
may allow investors to extract 75 to 80 percent of the equity in these
properties. This process involves refinancing the existing properties
at their current market value, paying off any outstanding mortgage
balance, and taking out the remaining equity as cash. This approach to
real estate investment offers a potent way to leverage assets for growth
while maintaining healthy yields. However, it requires meticulous
financial planning and market analysis to ensure that the extracted
equity is reinvested wisely and that portfolio growth does not come
at the expense of financial stability or investor returns.

For investors, this strategy represents an advanced level of
portfolio management, necessitating a deep understanding of market
dynamics, financing mechanisms, and investment risk. With the right
expertise and strategic oversight, leveraging equity through appraisal
and reinvestment can significantly enhance a real estate portfolio's
value and income-generating potential.

Hedge funds, REITs, and similar institutional investors have
developed sophisticated methods to replenish and grow their capital
reserves, ensuring a continuous flow of investment into their portfolios, particularly in sectors like single-family rentals and BTR developments. These strategies are rooted in a blend of traditional fundraising and modern financial technologies, including crowdfunding,
engaging accredited investors, and tapping into Wall Street resources.
The goal is to secure capital that can be deployed into high-yield real
estate assets, generating returns that exceed the promises made to their

investors. Here's a deeper dive into how these entities manage their capital replenishment and investment strategies.

Utilizing crowdfunding platforms that allow a large number of investors to contribute smaller amounts of capital is an approach that has become increasingly popular, offering a more accessible entry point for individuals to invest in real estate ventures traditionally dominated by institutional investors. Some hedge funds and REITs raise capital through public offerings or private placements, appealing to a broader range of investors, including other institutional entities, pension funds, and insurance companies. The strategies employed by hedge funds, REITs, and other institutional investors to replenish their capital and invest in high-yield real estate assets illustrate the sophisticated interplay between fundraising, market analysis, and portfolio management. By leveraging a mix of crowdfunding, accredited investors, and institutional capital, these entities are able to continuously invest in properties that not only meet but exceed the returns promised to their investors, thereby ensuring the growth and stability of their real estate portfolios.

The BTR sector has witnessed significant growth and evolution, particularly among the largest players in the market, who have been actively acquiring single-family assets since the 2008–2009 financial crisis. This strategic accumulation of properties was not merely opportunistic; it laid the groundwork for a sophisticated, data-driven approach to real estate investment that has shaped the current landscape of the BTR market. Let's delve into how these foundational strategies have positioned major investors for success in the competitive BTR sector.

After the financial crisis, many large real estate investors recognized the potential in single-family homes as a stable and lucrative asset class. The postcrisis market offered unprecedented opportunities to acquire properties at significantly reduced prices, providing a high potential for long-term capital appreciation and rental income. By expanding into single-family homes, these investors diversified their real estate portfolios, spreading risk across different property types and geographic locations. The shift toward BTR developments represents a natural evolution for these investors, leveraging their accumulated knowledge, data, and operational infrastructure to tap into the growing demand for rental housing. The trajectory of large investors in the BTR sector reflects a strategic and data-driven approach to real estate investment, built on the foundations laid in the aftermath of the 2008–2009 financial crisis. Their early entry into single-family asset acquisition, coupled with the development of sophisticated models and extensive market research, has positioned them strongly in the competitive landscape of BTR development. As the sector continues to evolve, these investors are well equipped to capitalize on the growing demand for high-quality rental housing, driving the next wave of innovation and growth in the single-family market.

The BTR sector's popularity surge, particularly in Texas, underscores a significant shift in the real estate investment landscape, driven by institutional investors' growing interest in single-family homes. This trend is not just reshaping the housing market but also highlighting the challenges and opportunities inherent in meeting the demand for rental properties. The statistics from Texas, with institutional investors accounting for 28 percent of single-family home purchases in 2021, more than twice the national average, signal a pronounced institutional footprint in the state's real estate market.[8] The significant purchasing power of institutional investors can impact local housing markets, potentially driving up property prices and affecting affordability for traditional homebuyers. Despite the significant role of institutional investors in the Texas housing market, their holdings represent only a small fraction of the nationwide single-family rental homes. This suggests room for growth in the sector, but it also highlights the need for a balanced approach to ensure that the expansion of institutional investment in BTR does not come at the expense of housing affordability and community integrity.

Negotiating the Contract

Negotiating contracts for BTR developments involves a complex interplay between developers, investors, and, often, intermediaries or consultants. The process is inherently iterative, requiring open communication and flexibility to align the interests and expectations of all parties. The example below illuminates the typical steps and considerations involved in these negotiations, showcasing the balance between developers' capabilities and investors' requirements. Here's a breakdown of the negotiation process, highlighting key strategies and considerations.

Setting an expected absorption rate, such as ten homes per month, is crucial for forecasting the project's financial performance and aligning it with market demand. With that in mind, we put in the contract an absorption rate of ten homes per month, with a

---

8   Rachel Carlton and Jishnu Nair, "Increasing Investor Purchases of Single-Family Homes Contributing to Rise in Rentals across Houston," *Community Impact*, July 8, 2022, accessed July 8, 2022, https://communityimpact.com/houston/bay-area/city-county/2022/07/08/increasing-investor-purchases-of-single-family-homes-contributing-to-rise-in-rentals-across-houston/.

selection of property finishes and interior amenities. We work with the developer to ensure he can come up with an average sales price for every single home of the development. Then I run that sales price through the potential investor, they run their analytics, and then they let me know what they can pay per home. Or they might say the homes need to have another bedroom and bathroom, with certain finishes, and other amenities. I'll then take that back to the builder/developer and ask whether they can execute the investor's terms. If they say yes, we're good to go. If not, they give me terms to take back to the investor; for instance, they may want another $3,000 per home to put in appliances. We also build in a 10 to 15 percent fluctuation in terms. Negotiating a contract for a BTR development is a dynamic and multifaceted process that requires balancing the developer's capabilities with the investors' expectations and market demands. By employing strategies that emphasize flexibility, open communication, and expert input, parties can successfully negotiate terms that pave the way for a profitable and sustainable BTR project. This collaborative approach not only facilitates smoother negotiations but also lays the foundation for a successful partnership throughout the development process.

Here is some language from a typical BTR contract showing the breakdown of price and other terms.

Purchase Price Cost Allocation. The parties acknowledge that the total Purchase Price of $20,300,000.00 is based upon an individual price for each completed house of $290,000.00 per house. The Purchase Price is allocated as follows:

DESCRIPTION	PER UNIT
Land	$ 35,000
Site Development	$ 35,000
Vertical Development	$ 220,000
Total	$ 290,000

(f) As of the effective date hereof, it is anticipated that Seller shall construct seventy (70) houses. Should the number of houses that Seller can construct change, the Purchase Price shall be proportionately adjusted accordingly (i.e., if 69 homes constructed, then Purchase Price shall be $20,010,000.00).

(g) **Adjusted Purchase Price.** If after six (6) months after the Effective Date the Vertical Development material costs increase or decrease due to causes beyond the Seller's control, the parties agree to recalculate the Purchase Price as more specifically described below ("Adjusted Purchase Price") based on changes in the Constant Quality Laspeyres Price Index of New Single-Family Houses Under Construction ("Index2").

(h) The Adjusted Purchase Price shall be calculated by comparing the last entry posted to the Index seven (7) days prior to each Phase Closing, to the last entry posted to the Index prior to the Effective Date. The percentage change between the two Index entries, shall be multiplied by 88%, the product of which will be multiplied by the Vertical Development Price to determine the Adjusted Purchase Price. For example, if the Index entry is 160 at a January effective date, and the July Index entry is 162, (162-160)/160 = 1.25%; 1.25 * 88% = 1.1%; (1 + 1.1%) * $220,000 = $222,420. Seller agrees to take reasonable actions to mitigate any such increase in the Purchase Price and shall keep Buyer reasonably informed of such events and the impact on the Purchase Price.

For a BTR project to succeed, a clear and comprehensive understanding of the project's overall costs by the builder/developer is crucial before presenting the contract to investors. This foundational knowledge ensures that the project is financially viable, aligns with market expectations, and meets the investor's return requirements. Understanding the total project costs and securing the project against potential disruptions are foundational steps in the successful development of a BTR project. By employing thorough cost analysis and strategic risk management and maintaining open lines of communication with investors, developers can set the stage for a financially viable and risk-mitigated project that meets both the developer's and investors' objectives.

Now let's take a deeper dive into just what's involved in the entitlement process.

REMEMBER:

➡ Getting the right financial partner in line early in the process makes a difference in the project outcome.

➡ Institutional investors are well positioned to finance BTR developments.

➡ Private equity partners can act like a bank to provide working capital, bridge loans, and mezzanine funding.

➡ Other ways BTRs are funded include through family offices, crowdfunding, and REITs.

ENTITLEMENTS

In the realm of real estate development, the journey toward creating a thriving build-to-rent community is multifaceted and meticulously planned. One of the crucial stages in this process is the "entitlement phase." This chapter delves into the significance of the entitlement phase, outlining its purpose, its key components, and the crucial steps involved in navigating this critical stage of development. This is a foundational process of any development, and it is crucial to have an experienced team leading this step of the development process.

Understanding the Entitlement Phase

The entitlement phase marks the initial step in transforming a vision for a build-to-rent community into a tangible reality. It is a comprehensive and intricate process that requires gaining the necessary approvals, permits, and permissions from various governmental bodies, local authorities, and other stakeholders to move forward with the development. Without successfully navigating this process, the development cannot move forward, and the investors and developers' soft cost will be lost.

The primary objective of this phase is to secure the legal right to proceed with the planned build-to-rent community project. It involves navigating a complex web of regulations, zoning laws, environmental considerations, and community engagement to gain the necessary green lights for construction.

Key Components of the Entitlement Phase

There are several factors that also can contribute to the time frame for completing the entitlement phase.

Feasibility studies and site evaluation: Before initiating the entitlement process, developers conduct comprehensive feasibility studies and site evaluations. These assessments analyze factors such as site location, environmental impact, infrastructure requirements, and market demand. The findings from these studies inform the overall development strategy and are essential in presenting a well-grounded case during the entitlement process.

Community engagement and stakeholder consultation: An essential aspect of the entitlement phase is community engagement and consultation with stakeholders. This involves reaching out to local residents, neighborhood associations, and relevant interest groups to gather feedback and address concerns. Transparent communication fosters goodwill and may lead to necessary modifications to the project, which could enhance community acceptance.

Zoning and land use approvals: During this stage, developers work closely with local government authorities to secure the required zoning and land use approvals. Zoning regulations dictate what type of developments can be constructed on specific parcels of land. Developers may need to request rezoning or amendments to existing zoning laws to align with the build-to-rent community's vision. In Texas this causes delays getting approval on minimal lot size requirements to sustain these developments.

Environmental impact assessments: Assessing the environmental impact of the proposed development is a critical component of the entitlement phase. This involves studies on the potential effects on the surrounding environment, wildlife, and natural resources. Developers must comply with environmental regulations and demonstrate their commitment to minimizing adverse effects.

Permits and entitlement acquisition: Securing the necessary permits and entitlements is the ultimate goal of the entitlement phase. These may include building permits, construction licenses, and approvals related to infrastructure, utilities, and public services. The acquisition of these permissions allows developers to proceed with the build-to-rent community's construction and development.

Navigating the Entitlement Process

The entitlement phase is a rigorous and time-consuming process, often involving collaboration with various consultants, attorneys, and experts. The steps involved in navigating this phase include:

1. **Preparing comprehensive documentation:** Developers must prepare thorough documentation that includes architectural plans, environmental impact reports, traffic studies, financial projections, and community feedback summaries. These documents form the basis of the entitlement application and are crucial in presenting a compelling case to regulatory authorities.

2. **Engaging in open communication:** Throughout the entitlement phase, open and transparent communication with local communities, government officials, and stakeholders is vital. Developers should actively address concerns, listen to feedback, and make necessary adjustments to the project to align with the interests of the community.

3. **Advocating for the project:** Developers and their teams often need to attend public hearings and meetings to advocate for the build-to-rent community project. Presentations, public discussions, and addressing potential opposition are part of the process to gain support for the development.

Input from Jason Hassenstab, Managing Partner

Since Managing Partner Jason Hassenstab handles the entitlement process, I asked him to share some additional insights. The rest of this chapter contains his input.

With the entitlement process, we move beyond well-educated assumptions made as part of the feasibility and due diligence on the land, and we begin quantifying exactly what drawings are being produced and determining actual costs of installing infrastructure (horizontal construction) and the homes (vertical construction) in the development. The specific phases involved in the entitlement process vary but in general involve estimating the costs of the development as its design evolves based on the findings of the engineering studies.

During the entitlement process, the main developer for the project oversees the engineering estimates of the various components that will be installed to turn it into the BTR development. These reports are submitted to the local planning departments for review against the various zoning regulations, planning codes, and other laws that impact the development site. After the initial reviews, the plans are weighed against environmental impact, and then once it passes those hurdles, it may be sent to the community for public hearing.

There are a lot of moving parts during the entitlement process because of multiple jurisdictions involved in the approvals and, simultaneously, approval procedures between various departments and planning boards. For instance, in Houston, if flood detention is part of the site build, the Harris County Flood Control District will need to be involved. The Harris County Engineering Department will also need to perform inspections. The city must also approve the final plat of the site, and that will move in parallel with the discussions with the Harris County Flood Control District and the Harris County Engineering Department. Because the engineering of the site is not within the city's purview, the city is only concerned with the plat itself. It might approve the plat conditionally based on the blessings of the detention and drainage design by the Harris County Flood Control Board and the engineering by the Harris County Engineering Department. At that point, the plat is then approved. Because floodplains and wetlands are so difficult to deal with, we try to avoid them when choosing a site. Wetlands alone can extend the timeline for a project another four or more years because of all that's involved in working with them.

Members of the Team

Again, there are a lot of moving parts involved in the entitlement process, so it involves a number of professionals with specialized expertise. These include:

City or county engineer: An engineer on the governing entity's payroll. That governing entity might be a city or county, depending on where the site is located.

A MUD engineer: In Texas, if the site is a MUD, the engineer is usually a third-party consultant. The MUD hires a private engineer to facilitate the engineering for the MUD on a contract basis and billable hours similar to the way an attorney is structured. There are obviously a number of engineering firms in the Houston metro, some of which specialize in the MUD space. It can generally be favorable to use one of these contract MUD engineers because they already have a relationship with the MUD board. They meet on a monthly basis and have a consistent communication process between them. Of course, that engineer is highly familiar with the district itself, and what may or may not be possible, even on a high level, without conducting a large amount of analysis.

Civil engineer: The civil engineer designs and oversees the construction of the development's infrastructure: its roads, curbs, water and sewage systems, and other elements of the development that meet basic human needs.

Structural engineer: This professional focuses on the design of the development and its homes to ensure they can withstand long-term environmental stresses and pressures. They calculate loads and forces on the homes in order to design foundational and other elements to ensure they can withstand the vertical and horizontal loads that will be applied by the structure.

Architect: The architect designs the houses and any commercial spaces applicable to the project. This professional designs the look and feel of the project. Sometimes, we'll bring in the architects before the approvals are all completed on the site. Generally, once we know the basic lot size, they can begin working in parallel with the rest of the design. The same with the structural engineer. In fact, the structural engineer and the architect may be finished with the actual house designs months before the civil engineering is completed and approved; their functions do not drive the entitlements schedule.

Land planner: We like to work with someone who is more familiar with the urban design requirements, building setbacks, minimum size requirements, and so on. A land planner will even know details such as how many trees are required, how to build a nature path, the right line of sight on a turn radius, calculations for the mass grading of the site, and detention volumes for all of our underground utilities, including drainage, sewer, and water.

Surveyors: Surveys are a component throughout the entire entitlement process, from purchase of a property all the way through the back-end sale once development is complete. These professionals conduct surveys, collect data, and certify surveys. We sometimes use peer surveyors who have in-house land planning and platting services.

Other consultants: We also sometimes use consultants for specific components. For instance, we'll utilize energy consultants to look at the energy modeling of the structures that we're designing and building.

We use these professionals whether the project is inside the city limits or in what's known as the ETJ or extraterrestrial jurisdiction—basically, projects outside the city proper. In the ETJ, the City of Houston still has the final say on the way that a property is platted so we still get the city involved very early on in the process, all the way through to final plat approval and certification. But when we're working in the county, the entitlements and inspections process can be much more favorable. That's why, in general anywhere in the US, large-scale master plan developments are done in the suburbs of major metropolitan areas because they're often going to be less regulated as a whole, and therefore the cost is less, which makes the product more affordable for people. Hence, the suburban sprawl.

The Timeline

From time of land closing to full entitlement of a property is generally around twelve months. However, since the pandemic, we've found that the timeline for the entitlement process has progressively lengthened, especially when working in the Houston city limits. These days, it is taking much longer to get through the entire process. Where it used to take maybe six to nine months, with the scale of projects that we're currently involved in, which are in the ten- to twenty-acre range, entitlements are taking a minimum of twelve months to even two years.

Much of the longer timeline with the BTRs is because of a negative stigma around these single-family communities. Part of that is public perception, which is that these are low-income, tax-credit or Section 8 housing or some type of government-subsidized housing. In reality, that's not the case at all, regardless of the type of BTR. Certainly some BTRs are on the more affordable end—that's really the purpose of what we're doing in the Houston area, trying to bring in affordable housing for families, professionals, and other individuals. But BTRs are single-family homes that are not subsidized in any way via either local, state, or federal government. In general, these developments are on par with Class A multifamily housing developments that have amenities such as gyms, pools, clubhouses, and more.

Another factor contributing to the slowdown of the entitlement process is that, in Texas as a whole, there is a tremendous amount of activity everywhere, and we just have limited resources to do what we need to do, particularly on the design side. Even the designers that are a signatory to the MUDs that we work with are absolutely swamped with the workload right now, and finding more qualified people to handle the current workload, let alone continue to take on more, is certainly a challenge. We all want to service our clients better, but we literally don't have the bodies to do it at the moment, so we have to be very strategic in scheduling.

Coordinating Entitlements with Construction

The horizontal construction, or the infrastructure components (covered in the next chapter), can actually begin before all approvals are obtained. In fact, the main focus should always be on starting the horizontal construction because the vertical construction (the houses) cannot begin until the horizontal is completed. So the critical path of the design also focuses on the civil engineering—the drainage, utilities, and so on. That work can start before the houses are fully designed because there are usually a couple of months of actual horizontal construction before anything is ready for the process of approving the houses to begin. That is different than the approval process for the sitework and utilities. The approval of the houses can typically be done in fourteen days, whether in the city or the county. And those are designed based on lot size and building code requirements.

REMEMBER:

➡ The entitlement process determines what can be done to a certain site based on rules and regulations and on back-and-forth discussions with city planners and planning boards

➡ The entitlement process moves beyond well-educated assumptions made as part of the feasibility and begins determining actual costs of constructing the development.

➡ There are a lot of moving parts and team members involved in the entitlement process.

➡ The entitlement process can take from twelve months to two years.

CHAPTER 7

HORIZONTAL AND VERTICAL CONSTRUCTION

Most people understand the difference between horizontal and vertical development of a property. Horizontal involves the components of a piece of land that ready it for vertical construction. It's the sideways development, basically everything that goes in the ground or, as is often defined, the structures that take up more space because they are longer and wider than they are tall. Also known as heavy civil construction, horizontal construction typically includes earthwork; transportation infrastructure, including access roads, streets, curbs, bridges; utilities (water and sewer lines, electrical, and gas); and landscaping elements (retaining ponds, walking paths). All of these are installed in advance of the vertical construction. Vertical encompasses the houses, garages, or other upright elements that make up the BTR community.

Environmental Concerns

Before horizontal construction can begin, any concerns unearthed by the environmental studies or soil tests conducted during the feasibility period are addressed. Although the land owner should be able to disclose if there was a business such as a gas station or dry cleaner on the site previously, which may be a concern because of how chemicals were disposed on the property, the environmental reports let us know the basic composition of the soil and whether any type of remediation is needed. Those tests are very thorough and drill down into multiple layers, if needed, to discover where the contamination is located. The tests also let us know what measures are going to be necessary to remove that contaminated dirt, how much has to be removed, what kind of remediation is involved, and whether we can even develop on that property. Any remediation measures are undertaken before the horizontal construction begins.

Contract Elements for Horizontal and Vertical

Horizontal and vertical construction plans are designed as part of the entitlement process. Most of the time, the developer already has an approved site plan through engineering before we go under contract with the investment group. That approved site plan, or engineering report, may still be pending approved permits from the city, so there will be verbiage in the contract that states that this is for that approved site plan. There are many changes that can either negate the contract or open up the discussion to restructure the contract.

Here is some verbiage from a typical BTR contract that demonstrates how both parties are protected.

$3,070,000 (Deposit) / 70 (Houses) = $43,857.15 to be credited per House at each Phase Closing.

Purchase Price Cost Allocation. The parties acknowledge that the total Purchase Price of $20,300,000.00 is based upon an individual price for each completed house of $290,000.00 per house. The Purchase Price is allocated as follows:

DESCRIPTION	PER UNIT
Land	$ 35,000
Site Development	$ 35,000
Vertical Development	$ 220,000
Total	$ 290,000

(f) As of the effective date hereof, it is anticipated that Seller shall construct seventy (70) houses. Should the number of houses that Seller can construct change, the Purchase Price shall be proportionately adjusted accordingly (i.e., if 69 homes constructed, then Purchase Price shall be $20,010,000.00).

(g) Adjusted Purchase Price. If after six (6) months after the Effective Date the Vertical Development material costs increase or decrease due to causes beyond the Seller's control, the parties agree to recalculate the Purchase Price as more specifically described below ("Adjusted Purchase Price") based on changes in the Constant Quality Laspeyres Price Index of New Single-Family Houses Under Construction ("Index2").

(h) The Adjusted Purchase Price shall be calculated by comparing the last entry posted to the Index seven (7) days prior to each Phase Closing, to the last entry posted to the Index prior to the Effective Date. The percentage change between the two Index entries, shall be multiplied by 88%, the product of which will be multiplied by the Vertical Development Price to determine the Adjusted Purchase Price. For example, if the Index entry is 160 at a January effective date, and the July Index entry is 162, (162-160)/160 = 1.25%; 1.25 * 88% = 1.1%; (1 + 1.1%) * $220,000 = $222,420. Seller agrees to take reasonable actions to mitigate any such increase in the Purchase Price and shall keep Buyer reasonably informed of such events and the impact on the Purchase Price.

One of the unique aspects of working with hedge funds is that they allow flexibility and pricing, as demonstrated by the percentage breakdown in the above wording. This is helpful if, for instance, it takes a year to build the development, and lumber prices increase again. The contract allows the developer to add those additional construction costs to the contract.

Costs of Horizontal Development

The costs for horizontal construction to develop the BTR site can vary dramatically depending on the conditions of the site, its location, and any work that has already been done by the seller. For instance, a site with a steep grade, poor drainage, high permitting costs, impact fees, or easements, may cost more than $100,000 to develop prior to constructing homes on the site. Conversely, a site that has been cleared and graded, and already has the main city and sewer lines laid, can cost considerably less.

The cost per lot currently is around $1,200 for water, sewer, fiber optic, and internet. Those are typical installation and connection fees for lots that already have utilities in place. If city utilities have to be brought in, especially from a distance—for instance, a mile-long water line has to be laid to provide access—then the costs go up dramatically.

TYPICAL SITE DEVELOPMENT COSTS (assuming no well water or septic system)	
DESCRIPTION	**APPROXIMATE PRICE**
Permitting & fees	
Building, inspection, certificate of occupancy (CO)	$300–$5,000
Impact fee (if charged)	$5,000–$25,000
Driveway (per house)	$50–$500
Municipal water & sewer (includes trenching, piping, tap fees)	
Water	$700–$20,000
Sewer	$1,000–$15,000
Utilities	
Electrical connections	$1,000–$5,000
Fiber optic (phone, internet, WiFi)	
Survey	$300–$3,000
Engineering inspection	$0–$1,000
Land clearing	$0
Earthwork	
Grading, rough to final for a typical site	$2,500–$5,000
Grading, cut, fill for a steep site	$1,000–$5,000
Site drainage	$1,000–$5,000
Retaining walls, if needed. Price is per square foot of wall face	$20–$50
Paving (asphalt or concrete)	$3,000–$10,000
Landscaping	$3,000–$20,000
TOTAL	**$18,870–$122,090**

Source: Adapted from BuildingAdvisor.com, Typical Site Development Costs, accessed February 25, 2024, https://buildingadvisor.com/buying-land/budgeting/typical-site-development-costs/.

Timeline and Team

The horizontal phase of a development for a seventy- to one-hundred-home BTR typically takes about six months to install streets and roads. If it's a smaller development, such as a fifty-unit BTR, it may take only three or four months.

With the partners that we work with, the builder and developer are the same company. So they put in all of the horizontal development, and they construct the houses as well (the vertical construction). Most institutional investors want the developer and builder to be the same, and then they just buy the end product ready for occupancy, or CO (certificate of occupancy) as discussed previously.

But there are companies out there with their own vertical construction contractors, so they want to capture that spread or profit, and they want to be able to do the construction themselves. We work with those investors as well, in which case the horizontal construction is done and the "shovel-ready" lots are sold to the investment group, which will use its own vertical construction team to complete the project.

Vertical Construction

As I mentioned, the vertical construction includes the homes themselves. These are very nice homes in the $175K to $400K range, for renters who will pay around the same monthly rent that they would pay for an apartment in the city. With the BTR community, however, they're getting a front yard and backyard, a garage, and more—a place to really call home.

Yet there is the perception that BTRs are Section 8 or some type of subsidized housing, and that by definition makes the quality of the homes inferior. That's simply not true.

All BTR homes are all constructed of the same quality as any other structure; these assets are built to last so that they can provide long-term, stable income streams for several decades. The same details go into a house whether it's a $300,000 house or a $2 million house. The construction details such as framing, studs, plumbing, and gas and electric lines are standard across the industry.

Granted, different materials may be used depending on the end use—a homebuyer who is planning to live in the house may want higher-end woods, cabinets, floors, finishes, and so on—and that is part of what determines the difference in the cost of a house. But again, in these BTR houses, we use materials such as laminate flooring and granite or marble countertops in the kitchen and master bath. Energy ratings may be higher in some homes—again, factoring into the cost of a home. But as far as the quality of the build, it is consistent with the standards established through the International Building Code (IBC), which is the standard used by most jurisdictions in the US. The IBC addresses health and safety standards for buildings based on strict performance-related requirements.

Builders build homes to withstand the external elements and lifestyles of those who inhabit those properties for decades to come. Market forces dictate that builders create quality homes; a builder that purposely builds an inferior product doesn't stay in business for long.

BTR homes are built with a one-year structural warranty from the date of closing, and that includes materials, labor, and crafts-manship—basically anything visible. There is a two-year warranty on systems, including plumbing and electrical—basically those unseen elements inside the walls of the structure. The foundation carries a ten-year structural warranty to cover issues such as settling.

Managing Inspections

Inspections are performed on the land and the construction of the homes. While the majority of inspections occur after construction has begun, some inspections take place during the entitlement phase as part of preplanning.

In Houston, a very simple single-family home will require around twenty inspections minimum, but that can go as high as forty or more inspections. For example, if the house is in a flood zone, there are another three or four inspections alone. Stucco adds four more inspections, and so on. The design really dictates the number of inspections. There are multiple inspections on the foundation, the framing, the insulation, the drywall, electrical, HVAC, and more.

Location also determines the number of inspections. The same house that might require a minimum of twenty inspections in the city will require only three in the county. This is why so many master-planned communities are being built in suburban areas.

Inspections are why the same house built in the county may take only three or four months to build where it will take seven or eight months to build in the city. Construction cannot continue on a property until the work that's been done has been inspected. And while waiting on the inspection, the crew is on standby. Fortunately, with technology today, the schedules can be better coordinated, allowing the inspections to be more effectively coordinated. Still, all those inspections and all the wait time in between adds to the cost of the home, which is why the same house in the city costs more.

It's a balancing act to schedule inspections on more than one property. But when we're building on a larger scale, we also get economies of scale, so we can get the inspections on as many as ten units at a time. And again, in the county, with only three total inspections throughout the entire build, it's a much more efficient process.

With BTR projects, we can also be more productive because the crew can work on several housing sites, then, while those are being inspected, move on to other housing sites.

On the BTR projects, currently, we're starting ten units per month, and each phase or tranche takes four months. So by the time the fourth phase is starting, we're nearing completion on the first tranche. Most of these BTR developments are in the seventy-unit range. With a seventy-unit BTR, there are seven total phases with four-month builds per phase. That means we will have built out all the houses within about a twelve-month period.

PHASE	NUMBER OF HOUSES*
Phase 1	Not to exceed 4
Phase 2	Not to exceed 10
Phase 3	Not to exceed 10
Phase 4	Not to exceed 10
Phase 5	Not to exceed 10
Phase 6	Not to exceed 10
Phase 7	All remaining houses constructed by seller in the project

"Horizontal" Housing Types in BTR

With BTR, horizontal can also refer to the types of housing, as in townhomes and apartments, and variations of these. In BTRs, horizontal apartments are basically townhomes. The unit is known as a horizontal apartment because of subdividing restrictions. For example, let's say a developer wants to subdivide a piece of land between individual (single-family) homes and townhomes, but the city does not allow that kind of zoning. So to get around that restriction, the developer just builds one large piece of land and can only sell that property as one unit, almost like a big commercial space. These BTRs are townhomes that are joined together with small yards in the back. That then eliminates the units being individually resold to consumers as an exit strategy, because there is only one legal address for the entire property, instead of 123 Main, 124 Main, and so on. I'll talk more about exit strategies in chapter 10.

Funding BTR Horizontal and Vertical

Funding for BTR horizontal and vertical components is different than with a traditional type of development. Horizontal components tend to rely more on state and municipal types of funding, since they are heavy civil construction projects. These components of the development often involve structural or civil engineers, and the quality of the project comes down to relationships with related industries. For instance, an engineer may have a strong relationship with a certain developer, who has strong relationships with certain electrical contractors because of their ability to deliver.

Funding for the vertical part of a project comes from the private sector (see chapter 5 for more information on funding). These components are typically driven more by architectural firms.

Some states may have special issues with land, but in Houston, where I operate, there is no zoning—that's why you may see a high-rise in a subdivision. Depending on the use, you can apply for a variance, which means that you're repurposing something that was commercial into a residential development, or it might be turning industrial into a multifamily or single-family development. Turning a single-family residence into townhomes by subdividing a lot also has to go through a variance.

What's unique in Texas, as I've mentioned, are the MUD districts that reimburse for infrastructure that is put in. Every state has certain opportunity zones that allow developers to defer some of their capital gains. If, for instance, you're holding a site for five years in an opportunity zone, you have a tax deferment or shelter on any of your capital gains profits.

Now let's look at some of the other gains from investing in the BTR space.

REMEMBER:

➡ Horizontal involves the components of a piece of land that ready it for vertical construction.

➡ Vertical construction pertains to the homes, garages, and other upright pieces of the development.

➡ Because horizontal construction may begin before all site plans are approved, contracts contain language to protect all parties involved.

➡ Costs of horizontal development can vary depending on the conditions of the site, its location, and any work that has already been done by the seller.

➡ Horizontal construction typically takes from three to six months, depending on the number of units in the development.

➡ BTR homes are constructed with the standards established through the International Building Code (IBC), which addresses health and safety standards based on strict performance-related requirements.

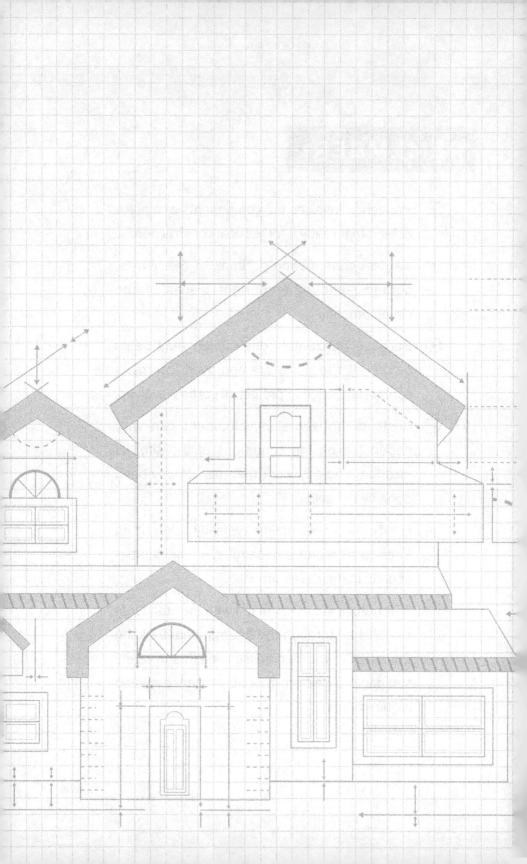

CHAPTER 8

EXPECTED RETURNS AND ABSORPTION RATES

A nuanced shift in investment strategies concerning BTR properties is that, unlike traditional real estate investments, where profitability hinges on selling a property for more than its development and construction costs, BTR investments generate returns from the onset. Here, the investor does not aim to make a profit through the sale of the property. For instance, consider a development where the total investment in land and construction might amount to $350,000. In a conventional scenario, this property would need to be sold for more than $350,000 to realize a profit. However, in a BTR model, the same property, costing $350,000, is rented out for approximately $2,500-plus per month, establishing a continual income stream.

The essence of optimizing returns in BTR investments lies in the clarity and foresight of the strategy. It's crucial that the properties are built to endure, specifically with BTR operations in mind, ensuring longevity and reducing maintenance over time. Additionally, incorporating a well-considered exit strategy from the outset is vital. These strategies collectively minimize long-term operational costs and maximize investment returns.

When evaluating a BTR, we look at it from a capitalization rate (cap rate), and then exit strategies, which I'll talk about in chapter 10. The cap rate is a measure of the expected rate of return on a real estate investment property.[9]

As I mentioned in chapter 2, the cap rate basic equation is:

Rent x 12 – HOA and taxes / sales price = gross cap rate

But there is another way to figure cap rate, which is the net cap rate. Every company, whether it's institutional that's doing acquisition on an individual basis, or a company that's doing a BTR cap rate, analyzes its net cap rate differently. So even though there's a general rule of a gross cap rate, every institutional investor has their own ideas of what to factor into a net cap rate. They may include factors such as vacancies, tax rates, and costs of insurance, property management, construction or rehab, or capital based on whether the property is cash or financed through some type of line of credit. For an institutional investor, a higher cap rate is best because that indicates a higher return on investment.

---

9   James Chen, "Capitalization Rate: Cap Rate Defined With Formula and Examples," *Investopedia*, updated December 22, 2023, accessed February 25, 2024, https://www.investopedia.com/terms/c/capitalizationrate.asp.

Return on Investment

On a national level, the average risk-adjusted annual return for BTR investments is approximately 8 percent, making it the highest return of eighteen property sectors tracked by securities advisory Green Street.[10] In 2021, around $30 billion in debt and equity was invested in BTRs. As of the writing of this chapter, the top investor groups were American Homes 4 Rents and Tricon Residential.[11]

Based on recent industry research and analyses, the SFR and BTR sectors have shown robust performance, particularly in Texas and other growing markets. In Texas, the BTR market is buoyed by several factors. There's no state income tax, and property taxes can be relatively lower compared to other high-demand states, which can enhance the net returns on investment properties. Additionally, the cost of building BTR properties can be lower due to the availability of land and favorable construction costs. The rents in major cities like Houston and Dallas are competitive and have been rising, reflecting the influx of new residents and the high demand for quality rental housing.

The performance metrics, such as rental yields and occupancy rates, have been strong in these regions. For instance, the typical cap rates (a measure of the annual return on investment assuming the property is bought with cash) in the BTR sector have been quoted at around 5.0 to 5.5 percent, indicating healthy returns.[12]

---

10   Will Parker, "Building and Renting Single-Family Homes Is Top-Performing Investment," *Wall Street Journal*, November 9, 2021, https://www.wsj.com/articles/building-and-renting-single-family-homes-is-top-performing-investment-11636453800.

11   Ibid.

12   "Single Family Build-to-Rent: Strategies Evolve with Rates Elevated and Supply Growth Accelerating," *Northmarq*, Special Report, December 2023, https://www.northmarq.com/sites/default/files/docs/NM%20BTR%20Report_Dec%202023_0.pdf.

Overall, while the specific figures like "double-digit net returns" of 10 or 12 percent may vary based on the exact location, property type, and management efficiency, the general trend in Texas suggests that BTR investments are performing well, offering solid returns underpinned by strong rental demand and favorable market conditions.

The BTR sector is currently recognized as one of the fastest-growing segments in the housing market, with substantial capital flowing into this area due to its promising returns. BTR investments can indeed begin generating profits relatively quickly, often within a few years after development, contingent on efficient execution and favorable market conditions. This rapid return on investment contrasts sharply with the timelines associated with traditional master-planned communities, which can take several years—from planning and development through entitlements and reimbursements—before becoming profitable.

The BTR market's growth is bolstered by high demand and robust investment activities despite a generally higher interest rate environment. This sector's appeal is further enhanced by its ability to offer quicker lease-up periods and maintain high occupancy rates, which contribute to a consistent cash flow. Moreover, BTR projects are attracting a wide range of institutional and private investors, driven by their potential for high returns and the continuous influx of tenants preferring rental accommodations due to various socioeconomic factors.

Absorption Rates

In evaluating absorption rates for BTR properties, the focus is on the rate at which newly constructed homes can be leased to tenants within a given period, such as one month. This metric assesses market demand by examining several factors: the number of available properties, the properties currently under contract (pending), and the properties that have successfully been leased in recent months.

For example, if a developer plans to build and lease one hundred homes, it is crucial to confirm that there are enough potential renters in the area to achieve full occupancy swiftly. Healthy market indicators might include a low number of active listings compared to a higher number of pending leases and a robust history of leases closed in the past six months to a year. Such a scenario suggests strong demand and a fast absorption rate.

Conversely, if the market has a high number of active listings relative to a few pending and even fewer recently closed leases, this indicates an oversupply of properties relative to demand. Such a condition, characterized by numerous available properties competing within the same price range and only a few low-priced properties under contract, points to a soft rental market with a low absorption rate. This situation suggests a declining market where properties outnumber interested renters, making it challenging to lease new units quickly.

When evaluating absorption rates, particularly for BTR communities, a key focus is the occupancy rates of nearby apartment complexes. If you're considering building a BTR community adjacent to established apartment complexes, understanding their occupancy rates is crucial. High occupancy rates, such as 90 percent or above, in these complexes can be a strong indicator of healthy demand in the area. This suggests that there is a robust rental market, which bodes well for the potential absorption rate of your new development.

If the neighboring complexes have a high occupancy rate, it implies that the existing tenant base is stable and potentially looking for upgrade options that a new BTR community might offer, such as enhanced amenities or more spacious accommodations. For instance, offering features like backyards, extra bedrooms, or a two-car garage at competitive prices can attract tenants from these existing complexes as well as draw new renters to the area.

It's important to analyze the broader rental market dynamics as well, such as the number of active listings, those pending lease, and the units successfully leased in recent times. A market with few active listings and high numbers of leases closed suggests a strong demand, leading to a potentially high absorption rate for new units. Conversely, if there are many active listings but few closures, this could indicate an oversupply in the market, signaling a lower absorption rate.

High absorption rates are crucial for minimizing holding costs, such as those incurred from units remaining unrented for long periods. These costs can significantly impact the ROI for BTR projects. Hence, understanding and strategically planning based on comprehensive market analysis and existing rental trends is vital for the success of BTR investments.[13] [14] [15] [16]

Let's look at absorption rates for one of the properties that we recently closed on.

13   Jeff Parsons, "Early Edition: 4Q23 U.S. Apartment Market Report," *RealPage*, https://www.realpage.com/storage/files/pages/reports/pdfs/2024/01/4q23-realpage-earlyedition-media.pdf.

14   Jeff Parsons, "Early Edition: 3Q23 U.S. Apartment Market Report," *RealPage*, https://www.realpage.com/storage/files/pages/reports/pdfs/2023/10/3q23-realpage-early-edition-media.pdf.

15   "Build-To-Rent: A Trend Fueled By The Pandemic And Interest Rates," *Integra Realty Resources, Inc. (IRR)*, 2023, https://www.irr.com/reports/IRR%20Viewpoint%20-%20Build-to-Rent%20Report%202023.pdf.

16   Olivia Bunescu, "Berkadia's Cautiously Optimistic Outlook for the BTR Sector," *Multi-Housing News*, January 25, 2023, https://www.multihousingnews.com/berkadias-cautiously-optimistic-outlook-for-the-btr-sector/.

PHASE	NUMBER OF HOUSES*	PHASE REAL PROPERTY (LOTS)	PURCHASE PRICE	CLOSING DATE
Phase 1	Not to exceed 4			
Phase 2	Not to exceed 10			
Phase 3	Not to exceed 10			
Phase 4	Not to exceed 10	Take the lots from the TRAC Map	$290,000/ house subject to adjustment as described above	Approx. 10 days after substantial completion of phase
Phase 5	Not to exceed 10			
Phase 6	Not to exceed 10			
Phase 7	All remaining houses constructed by seller in the project			

With Phase 1, four homes are built in the first month and ten homes each month thereafter. Those homes are delivered approximately ten days after completion. This BTR schedule is an extremely accelerated schedule; it's lightspeed compared to what a traditional developer would be able to manage on a housing development.

Absorption rate is also tied to the size of the development and waiting list of renters. For instance, if it's a one hundred home development, and there is a waiting list of one hundred renters, then the homes may be built much faster. Whereas, if the waiting list is only five renters long, then there might only be five or ten homes built per month. So the waiting list can also change the dynamic of how fast a community is developed.

The Waiting List

One of the keys to ROI is to have a waiting list of renters that lease the day of closing for each of the homes. In the ideal situation, we close on a property on one day and renters move in the next day, so security deposits along with the first month's rent and any prorations based on when they move in are already collected. That really is the catalyst for securing your ROI. As soon as the property closes and has certification of occupancy from the city—everything passes inspection and all utilities work—then the renter moves in so there is no burn rate on your investment, no vacancy to take out of your return on investment.

Typically, the marketing of the properties is done by the property management company that the institutional investment group owns or partners with. Most of the larger institutional investors own their own property management company, and those companies typically have a marketing and leasing arm. The marketing arm has multiple resources for renting the properties, one of which is online via the multiple listing service or MLS. The property management company also prequalifies all of the renters, often through a third-party service that performs background checks that include criminal history, employment verification, and any inconsistences in the application information provided by the potential tenant.

Usually the marketing begins as soon as the first phase of vertical launches. By that time, there is an online presence with renderings, videos, and signage at the site.

Determining Rental Rates

In the BTR market, rental rates are initially set based on current market conditions. However, if the properties do not lease as expected, it may be necessary to adjust the rates downward to enhance occupancy. For instance, if a property was expected to lease for $2,400 per month and fails to attract tenants, reducing the rent to $2,000 might be a strategic move to avoid vacancies and generate income, albeit at a reduced rate.

BTR investments typically aim for annual rent increases to align with market growth and inflation. Lease terms in BTR settings generally range from thirteen to eighteen months, though they can extend up to two years. Shorter leases less than a year are less common unless the local market is transient, such as areas popular with college students or single professionals.

Should market conditions improve and rental demand increase, landlords might then be able to raise rents. For example, if a tenant is currently paying $1,800 but market rates rise to $2,000, the landlord might incrementally increase the rent, although significant hikes might be challenging if the tenant has an ongoing lease. This strategy helps maximize returns while maintaining tenant relationships.

Overall, BTR properties are designed to offer flexibility in pricing and lease terms to adapt to market dynamics, ensuring that occupancy remains high and investment returns are optimized.

The ideal scenario in BTR investments involves securing reliable tenants who sign annual leases, with the ability to increase rents by a moderate percentage each year. However, expectations of an 8 to 10 percent annual rent increase are generally above the typical range observed in recent years. More realistic annual rent increases in the BTR sector range from 2 to 3 percent on average, although some areas have experienced higher increases due to specific market conditions.[17] [18]

Regarding the risk of market misjudgments by institutional investors, BTR investments are indeed subject to strict underwriting standards, which reduce the frequency of poor market assessments. These standards include thorough evaluations by lenders and internal teams, which help ensure that investments are sound, and neighborhoods are appropriately valued for development.[19]

In terms of development strategy, the focus is on selecting the right location and amenities that cater to the targeted demographic, whether millennials, mixed communities, or retirees. This approach is crucial for the success of the development, ensuring that the properties meet the specific needs and preferences of potential renters.[20]

---

17   Jessica Menefee, "What Is a Reasonable Rent Increase in 2024?," *iProperty Management*, November 30, 2023, https://ipropertymanagement.com/guides/what-is-reasonable-rent-increase.

18   "Single-Family Rental Investment Trends Report | Q3 2023," *Arbor*, https://arbor.com/wp-content/uploads/2023/08/Arbor_Single_Family_Invest_Rental_Report_2023-Q3_VF.pdf.

19   Menefee, "What Is a Reasonable Rent."

20   Ibid.

REMEMBER:

➡ The cap rate is a measure of the expected rate of return on a real estate investment property.

➡ The cap rate basic equation is: Rent x 12 – HOA and taxes / sales price = gross cap rate

➡ At this writing, the average risk-adjusted annual return for BTR investments is approximately 8 percent on a national level.

➡ Absorption rates refer to how fast the homes can be built and how quickly they can be rented out.

➡ A key factor in ROI is having a waiting list of renters that lease the day of closing for each of the homes.

➡ Rental rates are based on and supported by the market.

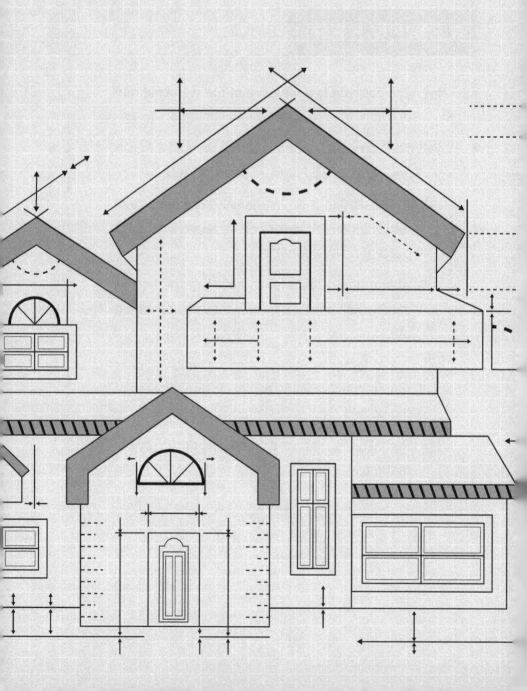

PART II:

LOOKING AROUND THE CORNER(STONE)

CHAPTER 9

STABILIZATION OF THE BUILD-TO-RENT COMMUNITY

Long-term success of BTR communities hinges on effective stabilization strategies. This chapter delves into the core strategies for stabilizing BTR communities, ensuring their sustainable growth, profitability, and appeal to a broad range of tenants.

Understanding Stabilization in Build-to-Rent

Stabilization in the context of BTR communities refers to the phase in which a property reaches a target operational and financial performance level, characterized by high occupancy rates, consistent rental income, and a strong community environment. Achieving stabilization is crucial for the long-term viability and success of BTR investments. Key indicators of stabilization include:

Occupancy rates: A primary indicator of stabilization is achieving and maintaining high occupancy rates, indicating strong demand and effective property management. In the third quarter of 2023, occupancy rates across all single-family rental property types averaged 94.4 percent, according to the US Census Bureau.[21]

Rental income stability: Consistent and predictable rental income streams are essential for operational stability. Even during recessionary periods, single-family rents have stayed positive, whereas apartment rents have seen a decline.

Tenant satisfaction: High levels of tenant satisfaction lead to longer lease terms and lower turnover rates. BTR communities often take the approach of offering Class A apartment lifestyle amenities supported by proactive marketing, on-site leasing experts, twenty-four-hour maintenance, and community amenities.[22]

Operational efficiency: Streamlined operations and cost efficiencies in property management and maintenance. Most of our institutional operators have an in-house management team to increase efficiency and profitability.

21   "Single-Family Rental Investment Trends Report | Q3 2023,"
     Arbor, https://arbor.com/wp-content/uploads/2023/08/
     Arbor_Single_Family_Invest_Rental_Report_2023-Q3_VF.pdf.

22   "Single-Family Rental & Build-to-Rent: The Emergence of a Leading Asset Class,"
     Berkadia, https://berkadia.com/wp-content/uploads/2023/12/single-family-rental-
     and-build-to-rent-market-overview.pdf.

Strategies for Stabilization

Stabilizing a BTR community is not without its challenges, including market fluctuations, tenant turnover, and operational inefficiencies. Developing a flexible strategy that can adapt to changing market conditions, focusing on tenant engagement, and investing in technology and innovation can help overcome these challenges. Here are some core strategies for stabilizing BTR communities to help ensure their growth, profitability, and long-term appeal to tenants.

Market analysis and positioning: Understanding the local market dynamics and positioning the BTR community accordingly is critical. This involves analyzing competitor offerings, local demand, and demographic trends to tailor the community's features, amenities, and pricing strategy to meet market needs.

Quality and amenities: Investing in high-quality construction and offering a range of amenities can differentiate a BTR community in a competitive market. Amenities that promote a sense of community, such as communal spaces, fitness centers, and pet-friendly policies, can enhance tenant satisfaction and retention. These amenities resonate with millennials that are just starting a family and usually have a pet. They also allow baby boomers and older demographics opportunities to move into a quality lifestyle community within their fixed cost of living.

Effective marketing and leasing strategies: Implementing effective marketing and leasing strategies is essential for attracting and retaining tenants. This includes leveraging digital marketing, virtual tours, and targeted advertising to reach potential tenants. Flexible leasing options and competitive pricing can also enhance appeal. Most of the BTR communities are comprised of over fifty units and have a full-time leasing staff.

Tenant experience and retention programs: Enhancing the tenant experience through exceptional customer service, community events, and responsive maintenance can improve satisfaction and retention. Implementing tenant retention programs, such as loyalty rewards or referral incentives, can further stabilize occupancy rates.

Financial management and optimization: Robust financial management practices, including efficient budgeting, rent collection processes, and cost control measures, are vital for achieving financial stability. Regular financial analysis and reporting can help in identifying trends, managing risks, and optimizing returns.

Sustainable practices: Incorporating sustainable building practices and green amenities can attract environmentally conscious tenants and contribute to long-term operational savings. Energy-efficient appliances, sustainable landscaping, and recycling programs can enhance the community's appeal and sustainability.

In summary, stabilization of BTR communities is a multifaceted process that requires a strategic approach to market analysis, tenant experience, financial management, and sustainability. By focusing on these key areas, developers and operators can ensure the long-term success and viability of their BTR investments. As the BTR sector continues to evolve, those who can effectively stabilize their communities will be well-positioned to capitalize on the growing demand for flexible, community-oriented rental options.

Occupancy Rates: The Cornerstone of Stabilization for Build-to-Rent Communities

Occupancy rates serve as a critical barometer for the health and stabilization of BTR communities. Achieving and maintaining high occupancy rates is essential for ensuring the financial viability and operational success of these developments. This section delves into the significance of occupancy rates, strategies to enhance them, and their impact on the stabilization process.

Financial stability: High occupancy rates directly translate to consistent rental income, which is crucial for covering operational costs, repaying development financing, and generating profits. They are a key determinant of the property's cash flow and its ability to meet financial obligations.

Market validation: Achieving high occupancy rates is also a form of market validation, indicating that the BTR community meets the needs and preferences of its target demographic. It suggests that the mix of amenities, pricing, and location appeals to potential renters.

Investor confidence: For investors and stakeholders, high occupancy rates signal the project's success and the effective management of the property. This can enhance investor confidence, facilitate future financing, and contribute to the overall valuation of the property.

Strategies to Enhance Occupancy Rates

The process of stabilizing a BTR community is deeply intertwined with achieving and maintaining high occupancy rates. Stabilization is not merely about reaching a high occupancy level but sustaining it over time to ensure continuous rental income and operational success. High occupancy rates, once achieved, must be maintained through ongoing efforts to enhance tenant satisfaction, market the community effectively, and adapt to changing market conditions.

Furthermore, the stabilization phase involves more than just reaching financial goals; it also encompasses creating a vibrant, thriving community that tenants are proud to call home. A focus on building a sense of community can lead to increased word-of-mouth referrals, further supporting high occupancy rates and stabilization. Strategies to enhance occupancy rates include:

Competitive market analysis: Conducting thorough market research to understand the competitive landscape helps in setting competitive rental prices and offering amenities that fill a gap in the market. Understanding what competitors offer allows BTR communities to position themselves uniquely in the market.

Targeted marketing efforts: Effective marketing strategies that highlight the unique selling points of the community, such as its amenities, location, and lifestyle benefits, can attract potential tenants. Digital marketing, social media presence, and community engagement events are powerful tools to increase visibility and interest.

Flexible leasing options: Offering flexible lease terms can appeal to a broader range of tenants, including those seeking short-term leases or customizable options. Flexibility can be a key differentiator in markets with high competition.

Exceptional tenant experience: Focusing on the tenant experience by providing responsive property management, maintaining the property to a high standard, and fostering a sense of community can lead to higher tenant satisfaction and retention rates, thereby stabilizing occupancy.

Incentive programs: Implementing incentive programs such as referral bonuses for current tenants who refer new renters, or offering the first month's rent free, can boost occupancy rates, especially during the initial leasing phase.

In conclusion, occupancy rates are a pivotal factor in the stabilization of BTR communities. Through strategic planning, targeted marketing, and a focus on tenant satisfaction, BTR developers and operators can achieve the high occupancy rates necessary for financial stability and long-term success.

Marketing During the Lease-Up Phase of Build-to-Rent Communities

The lease-up phase is a critical period for BTR communities. Effective marketing strategies are essential to attract tenants and achieve high occupancy rates swiftly. This phase sets the foundation for the community's financial performance and reputation in the market.

Here, we explore key marketing strategies and best practices for BTR communities during the lease-up phase.

The lease-up phase refers to the initial period of marketing and leasing a new BTR community until it reaches a stabilized occupancy level, typically around 90 to 95 percent. This phase is challenging due to the absence of a living community to showcase, making the marketing efforts pivotal in painting a picture of the lifestyle potential tenants can expect. Strategic marketing approaches include:

Brand development and positioning: Begin by establishing a strong brand identity for the BTR community. This includes developing a compelling narrative that highlights the unique value proposition of the community, such as its design, amenities, location, and the lifestyle it offers. Effective branding sets the community apart and creates an emotional connection with potential tenants.

Digital marketing and social media presence: Utilize digital marketing channels extensively. A well-designed website, virtual tours, high-quality images, and video content can significantly enhance online visibility. Social media platforms are powerful tools for engaging with potential tenants, showcasing community events, construction progress, and tenant testimonials.

Targeted advertising: Implement targeted advertising campaigns using demographic and psychographic data to reach potential tenants. Platforms like Google Ads, Facebook, and Instagram offer sophisticated targeting options to ensure your ads reach the right audience based on interests, behaviors, location, and more.

Community engagement and events: Organize events that invite potential tenants to experience the community, even before it is fully operational. Pop-up events, local partnerships, and involvement in community activities can generate buzz and foster a sense of belonging.

Incentive programs: Offering preleasing incentives can be a powerful tool to encourage early commitments. These might include discounted rent for the first few months, waived application fees, or free amenities for the first year. Ensure these incentives are prominently featured in marketing materials.

Leverage technology for virtual leasing: Given the increasing comfort with digital tools, offering virtual leasing options can broaden your reach. Virtual tours, online applications, and digital lease signing can make the leasing process more convenient for tenants, especially those relocating from afar.

Engage with real estate agents and relocation specialists: Building relationships with real estate agents and relocation specialists can help drive traffic to your BTR community. Offering incentives for agents who successfully lease units can motivate them to prioritize your community.

Measuring Success and Adjusting Strategies

Performance metrics: Track the performance of marketing campaigns through metrics such as website traffic, lead generation rates, conversion rates, and social media engagement. This data will help identify which strategies are most effective and where adjustments are needed.

Feedback loops: Implement mechanisms to collect feedback from prospective tenants during tours or events. Understanding their perceptions and objections can provide valuable insights for refining marketing messages and strategies.

In conclusion, marketing during the lease-up phase of BTR communities is both an art and a science, requiring a strategic blend of branding, digital engagement, targeted advertising, and community involvement. By effectively communicating the unique value proposition of the community and leveraging technology to reach and engage potential tenants, BTR developers and operators can successfully navigate the lease-up phase, setting the stage for long-term success and stability.

Pro Forma for Build-to-Rent Communities During Stabilization

A pro forma is an essential financial tool used in real estate development and investment, particularly for BTR communities. It provides a detailed projection of the property's financial performance over a specific period. During the stabilization phase, when a BTR community reaches its optimal operational and financial performance, the pro forma plays a crucial role in assessing its viability, managing expectations, and attracting investors. This section will elaborate on the key components and considerations of a pro forma for BTR communities during stabilization. Key components of a pro forma include:

REVENUE PROJECTIONS

Rental income: Estimate the total income from rent, considering the occupancy rates and market rental rates. This should account for the anticipated stabilization occupancy level, typically around 90 to 95 percent.

Other income: Project income from other sources, such as pet fees, parking, amenities (e.g., fitness center, event space rentals), and late fees. This diversifies income streams and provides a more comprehensive revenue outlook.

OPERATING EXPENSES

Property management: Costs associated with managing the property include salaries for on-site management staff, leasing office expenses, and property management software.

Maintenance and repairs: Regular maintenance costs to keep the community in top condition include landscaping, common area upkeep, and individual unit maintenance.

Utilities: These are the costs for common area utilities that are not reimbursed by tenants.

Marketing and advertising: These are expenses related to marketing the community and attracting tenants, which, as mentioned earlier, is especially relevant during the initial lease-up phase leading into stabilization.

Insurance and taxes: Property insurance and real estate taxes can vary based on location and property value.

CAPITAL EXPENDITURES

Improvements and upgrades: These are costs for significant improvements or upgrades to the property that enhance its value and appeal to tenants.

DEBT SERVICE

Mortgage payments: If the project is financed, the pro forma should include the cost of debt service, reflecting interest and principal payments on any loans.

CASH FLOW ANALYSIS

Net operating income (NOI): Calculate NOI by subtracting total operating expenses from total revenue. This figure does not include capital expenditures or debt service.

Cash flow before taxes (CFBT): Deduct debt service from NOI to determine the cash flow available before taxes.

Cash-on-cash return: This metric is critical for investors, calculated by dividing the CFBT by the initial equity investment. It measures the return on investment based solely on cash flow relative to the amount of equity invested.

Other Considerations During Stabilization

Market dynamics: Understand local market trends and how they impact rental rates and occupancy levels. This includes demographic shifts, employment trends, and competitor analysis.

Lease-up velocity: The rate at which units are leased can affect the stabilization timeline. Faster lease-up rates can lead to earlier stabilization, positively impacting financial projections.

Operational efficiency: As the community moves toward stabilization, it's crucial to streamline operations and reduce costs where possible without compromising the quality of services or tenant satisfaction.

In conclusion, creating a pro forma for BTR communities during the stabilization phase involves a comprehensive analysis of revenue, expenses, and cash flow. It must be adaptable to changing market conditions and operational realities. A well-constructed pro forma not only aids in financial planning and management but also serves as a valuable tool for attracting investment by demonstrating the project's potential for stable and profitable operation. As such, it's a fundamental component of the strategic planning and operational management of BTR communities, guiding them toward successful stabilization and long-term viability.

Management of Build-to-Rent Communities During the Stabilization Phase

The stabilization phase is a pivotal period in the lifecycle of BTR communities, marking the transition from the initial lease-up phase to achieving a steady state of operations, occupancy, and cash flow. Effective management during this phase is crucial for ensuring the long-term success and sustainability of the community. This section explores key strategies and considerations for managing BTR communities as they navigate through stabilization.

ACHIEVING OPTIMAL OCCUPANCY

Some ways to achieve optimal occupancy include:

Dynamic pricing strategies: Implement pricing strategies that are competitive yet flexible, allowing adjustments based on market demand, seasonality, and occupancy goals. Utilizing revenue management software can aid in making data-driven pricing decisions.

Targeted marketing and leasing: Continue aggressive marketing efforts to maintain visibility and attract new tenants. Tailor marketing messages to highlight the unique selling points of the community and the lifestyle it offers. Efficiently manage the leasing process to minimize vacancies and turnover time.

Tenant retention programs: Develop and implement tenant retention programs that encourage lease renewals. This could include offering incentives for renewing leases, conducting regular tenant satisfaction surveys, and addressing feedback promptly to improve the living experience.

FINANCIAL MANAGEMENT

Financial management strategies include:

Budgeting and cost control: Maintain strict control over operating expenses without compromising the quality of services. Regularly review and adjust budgets based on actual performance and forecasts.

Cash flow management: Monitor cash flow closely, ensuring that rental income is collected efficiently, and expenses are managed effectively. This includes setting aside reserves for maintenance, capital improvements, and unexpected costs.

Performance analysis: Regularly review financial performance against the pro forma projections. Analyze variances and identify areas for improvement or adjustment in strategy.

OPERATIONAL EXCELLENCE

Operational excellence involves keeping the homes and community in good condition to help maintain the value of the investment.

Property maintenance and upkeep: Ensure the property is well-maintained, with prompt attention to repairs and maintenance issues. A well-maintained property is critical for tenant satisfaction and retention.

Community engagement: Foster a sense of community among residents through events, activities, and communication. Engaged tenants are more likely to renew their leases and contribute to a positive living environment.

Technology integration: Utilize technology to streamline operations, enhance tenant services, and improve communication. This includes property management software, online payment systems, and digital communication platforms.

STRATEGIC FOCUS ON LONG-TERM GOALS

Long-term goals can help maintain the appeal of the community.

Sustainability initiatives: Implement sustainability practices and green initiatives that can reduce operational costs, appeal to environmentally conscious tenants, and contribute to the long-term viability of the community.

Market positioning: Continuously assess market positioning and adjust strategies to ensure the BTR community remains competitive and appealing to the target demographic.

Investor and stakeholder communications: Maintain transparent and regular communication with investors and stakeholders, providing updates on performance, challenges, and strategies for future growth.

In conclusion, managing BTR communities during the stabilization phase requires a multifaceted approach that balances the need for achieving occupancy and financial targets with the long-term vision for the community. It involves strategic pricing, effective marketing, financial discipline, operational efficiency, and a focus on tenant satisfaction and engagement. By navigating these challenges effectively, management can ensure the community not only stabilizes successfully but also lays a strong foundation for sustained success and growth.

Valuation of Build-to-Rent Communities During the Stabilization Phase

The stabilization phase of BTR communities is a critical juncture for valuation purposes. It marks the transition from initial lease-up and operational ramp-up to a period where the community achieves and maintains a steady state of operational efficiency, occupancy rates, and revenue generation. Valuation during this phase is crucial for developers, investors, and financial institutions because it influences refinancing decisions, investment returns, and the overall financial strategy for the property. This section delves into the factors affecting valuation, methodologies used, and considerations specific to the stabilization phase.

FACTORS AFFECTING VALUATION

Several factors affect valuation, including:

Occupancy rates: Achieving high occupancy rates is a key indicator of stabilization. Properties that quickly reach and maintain optimal occupancy levels are valued higher due to their demonstrated market demand and operational success.

Rental income: The amount of steady rental income generated is a critical component of valuation. Properties with higher, stable rental income streams are more attractive to investors.

Operating expenses: Efficient management of operating expenses without sacrificing service quality can positively affect net operating income (NOI), a crucial metric for valuation.

Market conditions: The local real estate market conditions, including supply and demand dynamics, rental rate trends, and economic factors, significantly influence valuation.

Property condition: The quality and condition of the physical asset, including its design, amenities, and maintenance status, plays a vital role in its valuation.

VALUATION METHODOLOGIES

Among the valuation methodologies for BTRs are:

Income approach: The most commonly used method for valuing BTR communities, particularly during stabilization, is the income approach. This method focuses on the NOI of the property and typically uses the capitalization rate (cap rate) to determine value. The formula is:

$$Value = NOI/Cap\ Rate$$

This approach highlights the importance of achieving stable rental income and efficient operations.

Comparable sales approach: While more commonly used in single-family or smaller multifamily properties, the comparable sales approach can provide context by comparing the subject property to similar BTR communities that were recently sold in the same market.

Cost approach: This method calculates what it would cost to replace the property minus depreciation, plus land value. It's less commonly used for stabilized BTR communities but can offer insights in markets lacking sales comparables or for newly constructed properties.

Other Considerations during Valuation

Lease-up achievement: The speed and efficiency with which a BTR community moves through the lease-up phase to reach stabilization can impact its valuation. Faster stabilization can lead to a reevaluation of the property's income potential and, hence, its value.

Stabilized NOI: For valuation purposes, investors and appraisers focus on the stabilized NOI, which is the NOI expected to be maintained after the property has reached its equilibrium occupancy and operational efficiency.

Market cap rates: The selection of an appropriate cap rate is critical and is influenced by market conditions, property location, and the risk profile of the asset. Cap rates can vary significantly across markets and property types, reflecting the perceived risk and expected return on investment.

Future growth projections: Projections of future rent growth, occupancy levels, and potential operational improvements can influence valuation. However, these projections must be realistic and grounded in market data to be credible to investors and appraisers.

In conclusion, valuing BTR communities during the stabilization phase is a complex process that requires a deep understanding of both the property's operational performance and broader market conditions. The income approach, focusing on NOI and cap rates, is central to this valuation. Achieving and maintaining stabilization is not just about reaching optimal occupancy; it's also about demonstrating the property's ability to generate consistent, sustainable income, which is crucial for maximizing its valuation. As such, the strategies employed during the stabilization phase can have a lasting impact on the property's market value and its attractiveness to current and potential investors.

REMEMBER:

- ➡ Stabilization is not merely about reaching a high occupancy level but sustaining it over time to ensure continuous rental income and operational success.

- ➡ High occupancy rates, once achieved, must be maintained through ongoing efforts to enhance tenant satisfaction, market the community effectively, and adapt to changing market conditions.

- ➡ When a BTR community reaches its optimal operational and financial performance, the pro forma plays a crucial role in assessing its viability, managing expectations, and attracting investors.

- ➡ During stabilization, the property management company will collect rents, provide reporting to the investment group, maintain the property's occupancy rate, and focus on keeping the homes in good condition.

- ➡ Achieving and maintaining stabilization is not just about reaching optimal occupancy; it's also about demonstrating the property's ability to generate consistent, sustainable income, which is crucial for maximizing its valuation.

CHAPTER 10

EXIT STRATEGIES FOR BTR COMMUNITIES

Investing in BTR communities involves not just the development and operational phases but also a well-thought-out exit strategy. The exit strategy is crucial for realizing the investment's value, maximizing returns, and mitigating risks. This chapter delves into the various exit strategies available for BTR community investments, discussing their implications, benefits, and considerations.

Overview of Exit Strategies

An exit strategy in the context of BTR communities refers to the plan implemented by the investors or developers to sell or otherwise dispose of their investment in the property. The choice of exit strategy depends on a multitude of factors, including market conditions, investment objectives, financial performance of the property, and the investors' risk tolerance. Some ways to exit a BTR include the following.

OUTRIGHT SALE

The most straightforward exit strategy is the outright sale of the BTR community. This can be executed once the property reaches stabilization, making it more attractive to potential buyers due to the demonstrated operational success and steady cash flow. BTR communities, especially larger ones, are attractive to institutional investors who seek stable, long-term income streams. The unique appeal of BTR communities for families or individuals desiring more space and privacy can command premium pricing.

> **Benefits:** Immediate realization of investment gains; liquidity.

> **Considerations:** Market conditions heavily influence sale price; capital gains tax implications.

REFINANCING

Refinancing involves replacing the existing mortgage with a new loan, typically under more favorable terms. This strategy allows investors to pull out equity built up in the property, which can be used to return capital to investors or reinvest in other projects.

> **Benefits:** Access to equity without selling; potential for lower interest rates and better loan terms.

> **Considerations:** Depends on interest rate environment and property's income stability; loan fees and potential for increased debt service requirements.

REAL ESTATE INVESTMENT TRUST (REIT)

Converting or selling the BTR community to a Real Estate Investment Trust (REIT) is another exit strategy. REITs are companies that own, operate, or finance income-generating real estate and are attractive due to their liquidity and dividend-paying structure.

Benefits: Access to a broader pool of investors; potential tax advantages.

Considerations: Requires alignment with REIT investment criteria; may involve relinquishing operational control.

PORTFOLIO SALE

Investors with multiple BTR properties may consider a portfolio sale, selling several assets to a single buyer. This approach can attract institutional investors or large-scale real estate investment companies.

Benefits: Simplifies the transaction process; potential for higher aggregate sale price.

Considerations: Limits buyer pool to those with significant capital; complex valuation and negotiation process.

SYNDICATION OR PARTNERSHIP DISSOLUTION

For BTR communities owned through syndication or partnerships, an exit strategy might involve dissolving the partnership or syndicate, redistributing the assets among the partners, or selling the property and dividing the proceeds.

Benefits: Flexibility in managing individual investment objectives; potential for direct return distribution.

Considerations: Requires agreement among all partners; potential for conflict or legal complications.

HOLD AND CONTINUE TO OPERATE

While not an exit in the traditional sense, choosing to hold the property and continue operations is a viable strategy, particularly if the property generates significant cash flow and has potential for appreciation. Depending on market conditions and the community's design, BTR properties may be sold as individual units to homeowners. This strategy can be particularly effective in markets with high demand for single-family homes but low supply.

Benefits: Ongoing income stream; potential for long-term value appreciation.

Considerations: Requires continued management and investment; exposure to market risks.

Strategic Considerations

Choosing the right exit strategy involves a comprehensive analysis of both internal and external factors. Internally, the financial performance, operational efficiency, and long-term prospects of the BTR community must be assessed. Externally, market conditions, investor sentiment, and economic trends play a crucial role in determining the most opportune time and method for exiting the investment.

In summary, selection of an exit strategy for a BTR community is a critical decision that impacts the realization of investment returns. Whether opting for an outright sale, refinancing, converting to a REIT, executing a portfolio sale, dissolving a partnership, or continuing to hold the property, each strategy comes with its unique set of benefits and considerations. Successful investors will carefully evaluate their options, align their exit strategy with their investment objectives, and adapt to changing market conditions to maximize their returns.

BTRs versus Traditional Multifamily Properties

The exit strategies for BTR communities versus traditional multifamily properties are similar due to their nature as income-generating real estate investments. However, differences in market positioning, tenant demographics, operational models, and investor perceptions can influence the selection and execution of exit strategies for each. Understanding these nuances is essential for investors to make informed decisions tailored to the specific characteristics and advantages of each property type.

Traditional multifamily properties typically consist of apartment buildings or complexes with multiple residential units. These properties appeal to a wide range of tenants, from singles and young professionals to small families. Exit strategies for traditional multifamily properties include:

Value-add and sale: A common strategy for multifamily properties involves making improvements or upgrades to increase the property's value and then selling at a higher price. This can include renovations, adding amenities, or improving operational efficiencies.

Sale to private investors: Multifamily properties, depending on their size, can be attractive to a broader range of investors, including private individuals, small investment groups, and family offices, providing flexibility in exit options.

Syndication: Owners of multifamily properties may opt to syndicate the property, selling shares to individual investors while potentially retaining a portion of the ownership and management responsibilities.

1031 exchange: Multifamily property investors often use a 1031 exchange as an exit strategy, allowing them to defer capital gains taxes by reinvesting the proceeds from the sale into another investment property.

Key Differences

There are a number of key differences when exiting a BTR. These include:

Market appeal: BTR communities often appeal to a different tenant base than traditional multifamily properties, influencing the type of investors interested in these properties at exit.

Operational complexity: BTR communities may present more operational complexities due to the nature of individual units, potentially affecting exit strategies that involve continuing operations.

Investment scale: The scale of investment and potential for portfolio sales can differ, with BTR communities often representing larger, more homogeneous investments that may attract institutional buyers.

Conversion potential: The potential for converting BTR units to individual ownership is unique compared to traditional multifamily properties, which are rarely subdivided in such a manner.

In summary, while there are overlapping exit strategies for BTR and traditional multifamily properties, the choice of strategy should consider the unique characteristics, tenant demographics, and market demand for each property type. Investors must weigh these factors against their investment goals, market conditions, and the operational model of the property to select the most advantageous exit path.

Parameters that Define an Exit

When defining an exit strategy for BTR communities, several key parameters must be considered to ensure the strategy aligns with investment objectives, market conditions, and the specific characteristics of the property. These parameters are crucial for maximizing returns, minimizing risks, and achieving the desired outcomes for investors and stakeholders. Here are the primary factors that define an exit strategy for BTR communities:

INVESTMENT HORIZON

Short-term vs. long-term: The intended duration of the investment plays a significant role in determining the exit strategy. Short-term investors might look for quick value-add opportunities and sell, whereas long-term investors may focus on cash flow generation and asset appreciation over time.

MARKET CONDITIONS

Economic climate: The general economic environment, including interest rates, inflation, and economic growth, can impact the timing and nature of the exit.

Real estate market dynamics: Local real estate market conditions, such as supply and demand, rental rate trends, and the competitive landscape, will influence the viability and timing of different exit strategies.

PROPERTY PERFORMANCE

Occupancy rates: High and stable occupancy rates indicate a successful BTR community and can make the property more attractive to potential buyers or investors.

Net operating income (NOI): The property's NOI, derived from rental income minus operating expenses, is a critical factor in assessing its value and the potential returns from an exit.

CAPITAL APPRECIATION POTENTIAL

Asset value growth: The potential for the property to appreciate in value over time can influence the decision to hold and continue operating the community versus selling it.

FINANCING STRUCTURE

Debt maturity: The terms and maturity of any existing financing on the property can dictate the timing of an exit, especially if refinancing options are considered.

Equity requirements: The amount of equity invested and the return requirements of equity investors will also shape exit strategy decisions.

TAX CONSIDERATIONS

Capital gains: Potential capital gains tax implications from selling the property can influence the exit strategy, including timing and structuring the sale.

1031 exchange opportunities: The possibility of deferring capital gains taxes through a 1031 exchange into another investment property may also be a factor.

INVESTOR AND STAKEHOLDER OBJECTIVES

Return on investment (ROI): The targeted ROI for investors and stakeholders will guide the choice of exit strategy to meet or exceed those financial goals.

Risk tolerance: The risk tolerance of the investors and their appetite for holding versus selling can impact the preferred exit pathway.

REGULATORY ENVIRONMENT

Zoning and land use: Local zoning laws and regulations can affect the potential uses of the property and its appeal to certain types of buyers or investors.

Legal and compliance issues: Ensuring compliance with all legal and regulatory requirements is essential for a smooth exit process.

In conclusion, defining an exit strategy for a BTR community involves a multifaceted analysis of these parameters to align with the investment's goals, mitigate risks, and capitalize on market opportunities. The strategy must be flexible enough to adapt to changing market conditions and property performance, ensuring the best possible outcome for investors and stakeholders.

REMEMBER:

→ One of the best benefits of the BTR asset class is the multiple exit strategies. These range from outright sale to refinancing, REITs, portfolio sale, syndication or partnerships, or hold and continue to operate.

→ Choosing the right exit strategy involves a comprehensive analysis of both internal factors, such as financial performance, operational efficiency, and long-term prospects of the community, while external factors include market conditions, investor sentiment, and economic trends.

→ Exit strategies for BTR communities versus traditional multifamily properties are similar, yet different. With BTRs, the key differences are market appeal, operational complexity, investment scale, and conversion potential.

CHAPTER 11

ASK CHARLIE (FAQS)

As someone heavily involved in the BTR segment, I often get questions from interested investors and individuals. Often, they are the same or similar questions, so I've included some of the key ones here.

QUESTION #1. Why has BTR grown in popularity in recent years?

There are a number of reasons. From the consumer side, one reason is the increase in the price of homes as rates have gone through the roof. A lack of inventory of homes available for sale has compounded the problem. For instance, as I write these words, in Houston, we currently only have two and one-half months of inventory, and everywhere there was a lot of competition and people were overpaying for homes. Lack of inventory is a big driver for BTR because people need someplace to live and are often being priced out of neighborhoods where they need to work and operate. BTR offers them an option for renting a nice home in a good location.

From the institutional capital perspective, there's a lot more access to financing. There is much more access to the various stages of financing: acquisition and development (A&D), vertical construction, and even agency (Fannie Mae and Freddie Mac) long-term debt sources have entered the picture, and they've come up with some very creative financing. The financing has increased availability to investor equity due to having a better understanding of the product.

Right now, the institutional partners that we work with are very particular on a location. Of course, that's the most important thing in real estate, and it's really driving decisions about locating BTRs.

QUESTION #2. What are some benefits of the increased interest in BTR?

In an economic downturn, it allows major players in the homebuilding industry who weren't able to get financing to build for sale to pivot to BTR and get financing and complete their projects. They're able to partner with institutional capital, whether it's a joint venture or co–general partner, or they're selling directly to the institutional investor at certified occupancy. So it allows them to not be handcuffed to a project where the bank won't finance them to build it and sell it. Now they can actually go back and replan it as a BTR.

It definitely provides real estate investors another avenue for investment properties. If you have five or six different institutional investors in one market, like Dallas, the competition for the single-family homes on the MLS and off market is pretty intense. BTR allows these institutional investors another avenue to invest in real estate. It's another big opportunity for them to increase their door count dramatically across the nation without having to buy single-family homes off of the MLS, through wholesalers, or through their off-market channels.

For consumers, the benefits of having BTR as an option is that they are newly built, high-quality homes with full amenities in safe neighborhoods. And they're built by big-name master plan builders like Lennar, Toll Brothers, Beazer, and David Weekley—not mom-and-pop builders. They're all building the same home, same product, same type of amenitized community. So consumers and investors are getting a really high-end product that will maintain and be easy to stabilize and won't deteriorate ten years down the road.

QUESTION #3. What features of a market make it ideal for a BTR community?

The ideal BTR areas are mature submarkets or suburbs of metropolitan areas; in Texas, that's basically anything within a forty-five-minute drive of a major metropolitan area like Houston or Dallas-Fort Worth. Some of the main factors that drive Class A BTR projects are proximity to good schools, access to downtown and/or work areas, access to quality retail and entertainment, and locations that are easily accessible to major highways. Markets where a lot of people are relocating are huge drivers of BTR. Chapter 3 discusses some of the factors to look for when identifying the ideal BTR community site.

QUESTION #4. Location-wise, where are you seeing the most demand for BTR builds?

Many areas throughout the country provide the right environment for BTR; however, we are seeing the most demand throughout the Sun Belt States (California, Arizona, Texas, Georgia, Tennessee, Florida, the Carolinas, and several others)—places where people are relocating and there is a lack of housing inventory. Obviously weather is likely a driving factor in these areas—it's easier to build in areas where the weather doesn't cause delays. But also economy and taxes are driving some of the BTR interest and development, as are municipalities that are open to the BTR structure. The Sun Belt States just seem to be a little more forward thinking in what they embrace in terms of development opportunity, so there isn't a lot of pushback or delays caused by municipalities.

The bottom line is the cost of land. In states like Texas and the Carolinas, there's still opportunity to develop land at a price that meets the BTR metrics.

QUESTION #5. What types of tenants and what types of investors are best suited to BTRs?

In chapter 1, I talked about the type of people who typically tend to rent in a BTR community. To recap that discussion and more: BTRs are ideal for anyone who is not in a position to purchase right now. That includes business professionals, families requiring short-term housing needs while in transition from renting to purchasing, or other individuals that are seeking to save money for a house down payment or those needing some time to increase credit scores. Really, anyone looking to live in a safe environment, but who is not ready to purchase. In Houston, BTRs are ideal for families relocating to the area; they can rent a BTR while they shop around and before buying in a neighborhood they like. As I write these words, interest rates have made buying a home unaffordable for many people, so BTRs offer an option to live in a nice neighborhood close to schools, work, and other amenities without overextending to try to buy a home.

From an investment standpoint: REITs, hedge funds, and other institutional capital seeking quality long-term investments are typically interested in BTRs. BTRs allow them to reach their door count without investing in multifamily apartment complexes, which makes for a safer investment.

QUESTION #6. Are amenities important in BTR communities?

Shared amenities typically are a key component; however, not all projects provide them. They are provided based upon project size, return rates to investors, and having available space to provide them. Smaller BTRs don't need the amenities, they need affordability. Larger BTRs that are stabilized with a lot more rent coming in can afford to be more luxurious monetized communities.

For instance, if you're building a fifty- to seventy-home community, typically, there are no amenities because the institutional investor or the operator doesn't want the revolving cost. The only things you'll see in a smaller build are a detention pond, maybe a dog park or walking trail, because they want to keep the rent as low as possible and not have to pay HOA fees, which amenities typically require for maintenance.

However, communities with two or three hundred homes often have amenities like a clubhouse and a pool, which are driven by the size of the community and location. For instance, in Arizona, there are condo-style BTRs with swimming pools, volleyball courts, and other amenities that are going after a different demographic. If a community is going after a more vibrant, younger demographic like millennials, then it might amenitize with a gym and a pool with barbecue pits. If the target demographic is older residents who are downsizing or empty nesters, then there likely won't be amenities in order to keep the rents down for the consumer. These renters wouldn't even need a dog park—they have backyards for that. They don't need a pool when they can optionally drive to one nearby.

QUESTION #7: What are some barriers to consider with BTRs?

With BTRs, it's important to have a well-qualified borrower, meaning they have a lot of experience in development/construction and a strong balance sheet. Even if you have the best location in town, and $20 million in the bank, if you need another $10 million it will be almost impossible to get financing unless you have a track record. That's why institutional investors are partnering with big-name builders, the ones with a track record whom the banks are more eager to finance. That means, unfortunately, some smaller operators are getting pushed out of this space because they're not able to get financing. And then some of the larger institutional investors are holding back instead of moving forward with certified occupancy purchases because they just don't have any certainty around interest rates.

With these communities, the return on investment for investors is important, and so fluctuating interest rates and cost of capital really determine their ability to be able to continue to build and operate. Stabilized and low rates are optimal, and that means getting a stranglehold on interest rates and cost of capital; otherwise, projects will continue to delay as we've seen recently.

Another potential barrier is having access to land in desirable areas. God only made so much land—and he's not making anymore—so that's a barrier in some areas. There's only a certain amount of land in certain locations, so being able to find a viable project in an ideal location that has utilities and does not have restrictions against BTR communities is key to the success of one of these projects. Plus, the owner of the land must be willing to sell at a price that makes sense for you to develop a BTR project.

QUESTION #8: What industry resources are available to help institutional investors better understand how to meet BTR customers' expectations?

Several different groups offer training and services to assist individuals wanting to understand and eventually become BTR professionals. A couple of great examples are YARDI and John Burns. The latter of these is considered by many to be the industry leader in this aspect. This is just one of the technology companies that provides data and training. And the data is incredible. It gives you every single BTR project in the entire nation that is either completed, under contract, or basically in entitlement and already through permitting and planning. It's one of the most incredible resources I've seen. However, it does come with a substantial monthly fee just to have access to data such as operator, builder, whether the project is completed, rental rates, cap rates, and more.

I expect to see these kinds of resources grow in the next few years as more BTR projects are on the ground and running.

QUESTION #9. What do you see for the future of the BTR sector?

BTR will be a main contributor of quality new rental options for years to come. I feel strongly that the BTR sector of the real estate industry will continue to be the fastest-growing, outpacing industrial and multifamily, which have been the two hottest segments for some time. But BTR is here to stay and will be the fast-growing sector through at least 2025.

REMEMBER:

➡ BTR remains a viable investment opportunity and a viable opportunity for people who, for a number of reasons, are looking to rent rather than buy.

➡ In an economic downturn, BTR allows major players in the homebuilding industry who weren't able to get financing to build for sale to pivot and get financing and complete their projects.

➡ Some of the main factors that drive Class A BTR projects are proximity to good schools, access to downtown and/or work areas, access to quality retail and entertainment, and locations that are easily accessible to major highways.

➡ The highest areas of demand for BTR tend to be in the Sun Belt States—places where people are relocating and there is a lack of housing inventory.

CONCLUSION

As we look toward the future, BTR is poised to become an even more significant and transformative force in the real estate market. By 2025, BTR is expected to solidify its position as a mainstream investment class, driven by the increasing demand for high-quality rental housing and sustained favorable economic conditions.

For consumers, the future of BTR promises an enhanced living experience. Developments will continue to prioritize modern design, high-end amenities, and community-building features. Renters can expect greater flexibility, improved property management, and a focus on creating vibrant, cohesive communities that cater to a diverse range of lifestyles and needs. As technology advances, BTR properties will integrate smart home features and sustainable practices, offering residents convenience and environmentally conscious living options.

For investors, the outlook for BTR is equally promising. The sector will attract more institutional participation as investors recognize the potential for stable, long-term returns. Innovations in construction technology and property management will enhance efficiency and profitability, reducing costs and improving operational performance. Investors should anticipate a competitive market with diverse opportunities across various regions and demographics.

Moreover, supportive government policies and urbanization trends will continue to bolster the BTR market. Strategic site selection, effective risk management, and a deep understanding of market dynamics will be crucial for investors aiming to maximize their returns. By staying informed and adaptable, investors can capitalize on the evolving trends and emerging opportunities within the BTR sector.

I hope this book has equipped you with the knowledge and strategies needed to navigate this dynamic market successfully. As BTR continues to grow and evolve, both consumers and investors stand to benefit from the enhanced quality of living and robust investment opportunities it offers. The future of BTR is bright, and those who embrace its potential will be well positioned to thrive in this exciting and rapidly expanding market.